# PRO FOOTBALL TRIVIA
# QUARTERBACKS

### 300 QUESTIONS FOCUSED SOLELY ON FIELD GENERALS PAST AND PRESENT

TJ JOHNSON

Text copyright © 2025 TJ Johnson All rights reserved. This book or parts thereof may not be reproduced in any form, stored in any retrieval system, or transmitted in any form by any means – electronic, mechanical, photocopy, recording, or otherwise – without prior written permission of the publisher. All inquiries should be addressed to Brainality Sports, 931 10th Street, Suite 606, Modesto, CA 95354 or tj@rejuvinist.com.


Cover design: Dzhafir


ISBN: 979-8-9995059-1-0

*To mom and dad
Love everlasting*

## Table of Contents

Introduction ..................................................................... 1
1. Who Am I? .................................................................. 5
2. Two Truths and a Lie ................................................. 13
3. Quarterbacks By Jersey Number ............................. 21
4. All Shapes, Sizes and Abilities ................................. 29
5. Heismans, MVPs and Other Awards ....................... 33
6. Draft Selections ......................................................... 37
7. Post Season Performances ...................................... 43
8. Statistically Speaking ............................................... 49
9. "Name" That Quarterback ...................................... 55
10. One For Each Team ................................................ 59
11. Bonus Baby! ............................................................ 65
12. But Wait, There's More, A Lot More! .................... 71
ANSWERS ....................................................................... 77
Answers - Who Am I? .................................................... 78
Answers - Two Truths and a Lie ................................... 85
Answers - Quarterbacks By Jersey Number ............... 89
Answers - All Shapes, Sizes and Abilities .................... 95
Answers – Heismans, MVPs and Other Awards ........ 99
Answers - Draft Selections ......................................... 104

*Answers - Post Season Performances ...................................110*

*Answers - Statistically Speaking..........................................117*

*Answers - "Name" That Quarterback ................................123*

*Answers - One For Each Team ...........................................127*

*Answers - Bonus Baby!........................................................134*

*Answers – But Wait, There's More...A Lot More! ...............141*

*Acknowledgements ............................................................150*

*About the Author................................................................151*

## *Introduction*

Welcome to *Pro Football Trivia – Quarterbacks*, the greatest test of your knowledge about the most electrifying position in sports! Whether you're at the bar with your buddies, tailgating before the big game, or simply looking to impress your friends with your football prowess, this book is your pro quarterback go-to guide.

As a lifelong football fan, I still remember the thrill of watching the Packers Bart Starr follow Jerry Kramer into the end zone from the one to "sneak" past the Cowboys in the legendary Ice Bowl. That moment, ignited my passion for the game and for the quarterbacks who lead their teams to glory. Over the years, I've dived deep to uncover facts and stats that make the game even more exciting. Now, I want to share that passion with you!

What sets this trivia book apart? For starters, it's dedicated entirely to pro football quarterbacks – a celebration of the icons who have defined the game. But it's not just about the questions; it's about how I ask them. With chapters like "Who Am I?" and "Two

Truths and a Lie," I've crafted a unique trivia experience that will keep you guessing and engaged. Each chapter is designed to challenge your knowledge while also sparking lively debates and discussions with your friends.

This book is not just a collection of questions; it's an invitation to have fun, learn something new, and test you and your friends' quarterback knowledge. As you flip through the pages, you'll find 300 questions that will entertain and educate, whether you're a casual fan or a seasoned expert. So, grab your favorite team jersey, pour yourself a cold one, and get ready to tackle these challenging questions head-on!

*"The quarterback is an extension of the coach and has a certain type of swagger mentality, on and off the field."*

*#1 Cam Newton*

# 1. Who Am I?

Quarterbacks. There's just something special about them. In every quarterback's history there is something that all will recognize as a signature moment. Some of those moments are easily remembered, others are a little more hidden. Each of the following questions will begin with clues to aid one's memory. Based on the clues, can you name the QB?

1. I won the 2014 Heisman Trophy after throwing for 4,454 yards and rushing for 770 yards as a college senior. I was the 2nd overall player picked in my draft class. My first NFL post-season touchdown pass was to myself. **Who am I?**

2. I started 11 games as a college freshman…*for the men's basketball team*. I was a 9th round NFL draft pick. Early in my career I served as Warren Moon's backup. I even played a year in Europe for the London Monarchs. I won a Super Bowl as a starting

quarterback. And, oh yeah, I am the first quarterback to throw a touchdown pass to myself in NFL history. **Who am I?**

3.   I was an undrafted free agent out of Northeast Louisiana University. On November 14, 1993, while subbing for an injured Scott Mitchell, I led the winning touchdown drive for the Miami Dolphins resulting in coach Don Shula's record breaking 325th victory. I spent the bulk of my playing career as a backup to a Hall of Fame quarterback. I later became a head coach and made one of the gutsiest calls in Super Bowl history which helped us win it. **Who am I?**

4.   Among the awards I have won is NFL Comeback Player of the Year, NFL MVP and Super Bowl MVP (sadly, I did not win the Heisman Trophy). While I led one of the greatest comebacks in college football history, as well as a comeback for the ages in the Super Bowl, I do not crack the top 25 of the NFL Game-Winning Drives Career Leaders List (I am currently tied for 26th). I led the Kansas City Chiefs to their first AFC Championship game since 1970. **Who am I?**

5.   In college, I was a 2nd Team All American and my #8 jersey was retired by my school. In a 2001 game I threw for 531 yards against Michigan State, good enough for 3rd all-time on my college's single game passing yards list. My brother is number 2 on that same list. I became the overall #1 pick in the NFL draft, played for 4 different teams but never really recovered from my rookie year woes. That year I was sacked 76 times and recovered 12 of my own fumbles. I did have some bright spots however. I once threw 22 straight completions against the Buffalo Bills and I

do have a Super Bowl ring which I earned as a backup quarterback. **Who am I?**

6.  I was a 5th round draft pick of a team that I spent 16 years quarterbacking. I could do it all. I scored 12 rushing touchdowns in 1976 and in 1979 I led the NFL in touchdown passes with 28. I threw a touchdown pass in Super Bowl XX in a lopsided loss. I was known for my toughness and long remembered for the neck roll I wore in my later years. **Who am I?**

7.  I was the #1 overall pick of the NFL draft and had quick success making the Pro Bowl my second year after leading the NFL with 4,555 yards passing. I later signed a 10- year $103 million contract with the team only to get injured. No worries as I still got a Super Bowl ring. The year after I got injured, I left to play for a rival team, again making the Pro Bowl after throwing for 4,359 yards. I had a solid NFL career but I'm most well known for being the NFLs Wally Pipp thanks to a crushing blow by Mo Lewis. **Who am I?**

8.  Many remember that Alex Smith was picked #1 overall by the San Francisco Forty-Niners in the 2005 NFL draft and that Aaron Rodgers was selected late in that round by the Green Bay Packers. What many may not remember is that I was the other quarterback also selected in the first round with the very next pick after Aaron Rodgers. I played for 5 different teams including the Oakland Raiders who I had a 11-7 record with as a starter. **Who am I?**

9.  I was a 2nd round selection after coming out of the University of West Virginia but played only 4 years in the NFL. I

earned a law degree from the University of Texas and began a sports management career, eventually becoming CEO and Commissioner of the XFL only to be fired by owner Vince McMahon when the league filed for bankruptcy. Most will not know me but will sure remember my son who was a #1 overall pick and threw for more yards in his rookie season than I did in my whole career. **Who am I?**

10.    I am a Super Bowl champion, Super Bowl MVP, two-time NFL Offensive Player of the Year, and NFL Comeback Player of the Year. I've set many passing records including throwing a touchdown in 54 consecutive games. The Atlanta Falcons drafted Michael Vick ahead of me. Still don't know who I am? I'll give you a final hint: I also have 8 passing receptions. **Who am I?**

11.    I was a NFL first round draft pick. As a college freshman, I shared the quarterback room with a sophomore who was a future first round pick and a junior who was a future second round pick. Of the three of us, I had the best rookie season throwing for 3,801 yards, 22 touchdowns and 13 interceptions while being named to the Pro Bowl. My how times have changed! **Who am I?**

12.    Prior to my NFL career I played minor league baseball for the Tri-City Dust Devils and Asheville Tourists as a second baseman. While I wasn't drafted until the third round of the NFL draft, I tied the record for most touchdown passes by a rookie. Even though I'm a 10-time Pro-Bowler and Super Bowl Champion, I'll probably always be known for one particular interception I threw in a crucial situation. **Who am I?**

13.   I don't know what I need to do. In 2024 I threw for 4,320 yards while completing 70.4% of my passes. I led my team to a winning record while also leading four fourth quarter comebacks. After a season like this, not only did I not get a Pro Bowl nod, I got traded! **Who am I?**

14.   I entered the NFL an undrafted free agent from a small private liberal arts college in Wisconsin that no longer exists. I quarterbacked for 18 years in the NFL during the 80s and 90s for such teams as the Tennessee Oilers, Chicago Bears, Arizona Cardinals, Detroit Lions, Kansas City Chiefs and the Seattle Seahawks. I was a 3-time Pro Bowler and in 1991 I led the NFL in completion percentage. I'm best known as the quarterback that was sacked 9 times in one game, 7 by Derrick Thomas, whose record still stands today. What many forget however, is that on the last play of that game I threw a 25-yard touchdown pass that gave us the victory. **Who am I?**

15.   I am the first quarterback to win the Heisman Trophy, be the #1 overall draft pick and become a Super Bowl MVP. If it wasn't for the way my NFL career started, I might have been a Hall of Famer. **Who am I?**

16.   I was selected 25th in the first round by a team that already had a future Hall of Fame quarterback. I was with 3 teams in my first four years and started only 4 games. I struggled, in part, because I was only 20 years old when drafted. Clearly, I wasn't ready. Remember the XFL? Well, on my road back to the NFL I was the league's MVP in their only season of existence playing for the LA Xtreme. I also played in the Arena Football League for the New Jersey Red Dogs. During my second stint in the NFL, I won

Comeback Player of the Year and helped my team to the playoffs. **Who am I?**

17. I bet you've forgotten all about me. I was an 8th round draft pick who led LSU to a Tangerine Bowl win earning game MVP honors. In the NFL I am best known as the bridge between two Hall of Fame QBs, even though I, too, led the team to a Super Bowl appearance in the 80s (we lost to the Redskins 27-17). I was the youngest quarterback to start a Super Bowl at that time. The next season I struggled in the first several games. By the fifth game, my coach benched me in favor of a guy who became an all-time great Hall of Famer. **Who am I?**

18. You may have forgotten me too…unless you're a Giants or Eagles fan. I am one of only a few New Mexico State Aggie players to spend time in the NFL where I quarterbacked for 8 seasons after beginning my career with the Calgary Stampeders in the CFL. I am best known as the reason for the "victory formation" and quarterbacks "taking a knee" to end games today. **Who am I?**

19. I was a high school teammate of actor Forest Whitaker at Palisades High School. It's only fitting that I would go to UCLA and after 4 seasons with the Washington Redskins, eventually play for the L.A. Raiders for 5. I have a Super Bowl ring (thanks to Doug Williams) but I'm better known for being the QB who came in for Joe Theisman after he broke his leg against the New York Giants on November 18, 1985 and helped win the game. Speaking of catastrophic injuries, I was also the quarterback for the Raiders when Bo Jackson hurt his tip against the Cincinnati Bengals. **Who am I?**

20.     I'm another quarterback you may have forgotten. I played for 17 seasons in the NFL bouncing around the league with 6 different teams until I found a home with the Falcons. I made the Pro Bowl with them for two straight seasons. I led them to a 14-2 season and their first ever Super Bowl, SB XXXIII on January 31, 1999. We lost in what would be John Elway's last game, 34-19. **Who am I?**

*"There's nothing like having the ball in your hands in the fourth quarter and you've got two minutes to go…and you've got to go get a field goal or a touchdown."*

*#2 Matt Ryan*

## 2. Two Truths and a Lie

How well do you know quarterbacks? For each of the following, two statements will be truthful facts, the other statement is a lie. Your job is to figure out which statement is untrue. WARNING – these questions are difficult! Answer these correctly and you are indeed a QB historian! Which statement is the lie?

21.  **Two truths and a lie**: Which one of these statements about quarterback Neil Lomax is not true?
a.    By the time I left college I owned 90 collegiate records including throwing for 7 touchdowns in the first quarter of a game.
b.    I was the only quarterback selected within the first three rounds of the 1981 NFL draft; The St Louis Cardinals selected me in the second round with the 33rd pick.

c. I'm currently second all-time on the Cardinals career passing yardage list.

22. ***Two truths and a lie:*** Which one of these statements about quarterback Jeff Hostetler is not true?
a. I led the Giants to a 20-19 victory over the Buffalo Bills in Super Bowl XXV.
b. I blocked a punt in a 1986 game against the Philadelphia Eagles
c. I made the Pro Bowl 3 times with 3 different teams.

23. ***Two truths and a lie:*** Which one of these statements about Randall Cunningham is not true?
a. I had 20 punts in my career, averaging 44.7 yards.
b. In the 1988 Divisional Playoffs against the Chicago Bears which came to be known as the "Fog Bowl", I fumbled 3 times.
c. I took over as quarterback of the Dallas Cowboys during the 2000 season when Troy Aikman went down with his last concussion ending his career.

24. ***Two truths and a lie:*** Which one of these statements about Joe Montana is not true?
a. In my first Super Bowl (SB XVI against the Cincinnati Bengals) I was voted MVP even though I completed only 14 passes for 157 yards.
b. In 1979, my rookie year, I ran for 112 yards in a game against the Cowboys including a 64-yard touchdown.
c. When I played for the Kansas City Chiefs, I chose to wear jersey #19, not the #16 jersey that I wore in San Francisco.

25.  **Two truths and a lie:** Which one of these statements about Tony Romo is not true?

a.  I played fewer regular season games for the Cowboys than Troy Aikman but threw for more yards, more touchdowns and fewer interceptions than the Hall of Famer.

b.  I have won the American Century Championship celebrity golf tournament (Lake Tahoe) 3 times: 2018, 2019 and 2022.

c.  In Dallas Cowboys history I am second to Roger Staubach in career game winning drives and 4th quarter comebacks.

26.  **Two truths and a lie:** Which one of these statements about Mitchell Trubisky is not true?

a.  I was selected ahead of Patrick Mahomes and Deshaun Watson in the 2017 NFL draft even though I was only 3rd Team All ACC.

b.  Say what you will but going into the 2025 season I have a winning record as a starting quarterback, a 64% career completion percentage, and have even made the Pro Bowl.

c.  In my first year in Pittsburgh, I threw for 3 more touchdowns than in my rookie year in Chicago.

27.  **Two truths and a lie:** Which one of these statements about C.J. Stroud is not true?

a.  I am the second highest drafted quarterback in Ohio State history topped only by Justin Fields.

b.  In my 3 years at Ohio State, I was never able to beat Michigan.

c.  In my second year in the NFL, I had even more pass attempts as well as pass completions than I did in my Pro Bowl rookie season.

28.    **_Two truths and a lie:_** Which one of these statements about Justin Fields is not true?

a.    I saw action in 12 games as a freshman for the Georgia Bulldogs.

b.    In my first 4 seasons in the NFL, I've thrown 45 TDs but I've also turned the ball over 43 times (12 fumbles lost and 31 interceptions).

c.    In my one year in Pittsburgh I had my career lowest completion percentage, average yards per pass attempt and passer rating.

29.    **_Two truths and a lie._** Which one of these statements about Bo Nix is not true?

a.    I have played in 70 college football games throwing for more than 18,000 yards.

b.    In a 2024 game against the Baltimore Ravens, I caught a 2-yard touchdown pass from Courtland Sutton.

c.    I am the son of Pat Nix who played quarterback at Auburn and was their career passing efficiency leader by the end of his career.

30.    **_Two truths and a lie:_** Which one of these statements about Ben Roethlisberger is not true?

a.    I am the second youngest quarterback, behind Patrick Mahomes, to win a Super Bowl.

b.    I have thrown for more passing yards, made more playoff appearances and have a higher winning percentage than Eli Manning and Phillip Rivers, both of whom were selected higher than me in the 2004 draft.

c.    I played wide receiver in high school until my senior year when I became a quarterback.

31.    ***Two truths and a lie:*** Which one of these statements about Sam Bradford is not true?
a.    I was the second sophomore in history to win the Heisman Trophy.
b.    After being selected first overall by the St. Louis Rams in the 2010 NFL draft, I set a record for most completions in a season by a rookie and became Offensive Rookie of the Year.
c.    I wore jersey #8 for each NFL team I played for including the Rams, Vikings, Eagles and Cardinals.

32.    ***Two truths and a lie:*** Which one of these statements about Tim Tebow is not true?
a.    Say what you will about me and my NFL career stats but I have a winning record as an NFL starting quarterback, I've thrown more TDs than interceptions, and my average yards per pass completion is a lofty 14.0.
b.    In my 2009 season at Florida, I threw for 2,895 yards and 21 touchdowns, rushed for 910 yards scoring 14 touchdowns on the ground, had a 70.1% completion percentage, yet still did not win the Heisman Trophy. Instead, I placed 5th.
c.    In the NFL I didn't throw for as many yards or touchdowns as Sam Bradford who was drafted ahead of me, or Colt McCoy who was drafted after me, but at least I'm accurate. My completion percentage was higher than both of those guys.

33.    ***Two truths and a lie:*** Which one of these statements about Peyton Manning is not true?
a.    I have a comedic side to me. In fact, I've appeared on Saturday Night Live several times and even hosted the show once.

b.     The only award that my brother Eli has won that I haven't is NFL Comeback Player of the Year.
c.     Speaking of Awards, not only did I win 5 NFL MVP Awards, I was also voted 1st team All Pro more than twice as many times as Tom Brady.

34.    **_Two truths and a lie:_** Which one of these statements about Jared Goff is not true?
a.     My dad was a major league baseball player for the Expos, Pirates and Astros back in the early '90s.
b.     During my college career at Cal, I went 0-9 against in-state rivals Stanford, USC and UCLA.
c.     While with the Rams, I made two Pro Bowls but never cracked the 4,000 yards passing barrier in a season.

35.    **_Two truths and a lie:_** Which one of these statements about Jalen Hurts is not true?
a.     In the 2018 College Football Playoff National Championship game I got benched and replaced by Tua Tagovailoa who ultimately led the team to victory.
b.     After transferring to Oklahoma, I finished second in the Heisman Trophy voting to former teammate wide receiver DeVonta Smith who would soon become my teammate with the Eagles.
c.     I am the first Philadelphia Eagles quarterback to lead the team to two Super Bowls.

36.    **_Two truths and a lie:_** Which one of these statements about Sam Darnold is not true?
a.     I only started 24 games at USC and threw only 57 touchdowns before declaring for the draft.

b.     At 6'1" and 195 lbs, many scouts felt I was too small to excel at the NFL level.

c.     I finally had a breakout year in 2024 throwing for 4,319 yards and 35 touchdowns and made the Pro Bowl. But that Baker Mayfield, who was drafted ahead of me, got me again! He threw for 4,500 yards and 41 touchdowns while also making the Pro Bowl.

*"I truly believe in positive synergy, that your positive mindset gives you a more hopeful outlook, and belief that you can do something great means you will do something great."*

*#3 Russell Wilson*

# 3. Quarterbacks By Jersey Number

Close your eyes. If someone were to shout out "jersey number 12" who comes to mind? What about "jersey number 16"? Let's test your QB IQ based on some iconic (and not so iconic) jersey numbers. Ready? Let's go!

37.     Of the NFL quarterbacks who wore jersey number 10, who has thrown for more yards in his NFL career?

38.     Of the NFL quarterbacks who wore jersey number 15, who has thrown for more yards in his NFL career?

39.     Patrick Mahomes will likely be the second quarterback who wore jersey number 15 to be voted into the Hall of Fame. What jersey number did he wear in college?

## PRO FOOTBALL TRIVIA - QUARTERBACKS

40. Who was the first Super Bowl winning quarterback to wear jersey #15?

41. Of the NFL quarterbacks who wore jersey number 7 who has thrown for more yards in his NFL career?

42. All of the quarterbacks below who wore jersey number 9 in their NFL career. Which one threw for the most touchdowns?
a. Tony Romo
b. Steve McNair
c. Jim McMahon
d. Sonny Jurgensen

43. Of the following NFL quarterbacks who wore jersey number 11 which one does not have a Super Bowl ring either as a starter or as a backup?
a. Drew Bledsoe
b. Mark Rypien
c. Alex Smith
d. Danny White

44. Of the following NFL quarterbacks who wore jersey number 12 which one has the highest career passer rating?
a. Aaron Rodgers
b. Terry Bradshaw
c. Tom Brady
d. Roger Staubach

45. From 1970 through 1979, four quarterbacks ruled the NFL. All four wore jersey number 12. They are Terry Bradshaw, Roger Staubach, Bob Griese, and Ken Stabler. Each of the four

won 70% of the games they started. Which had the highest winning percentage, most passing yards and most touchdown passes during that 10-year stretch (NOTE: it's the same person for each)?

46.     Terry Bradshaw is known for winning 4 Super Bowls but also for throwing the "immaculate reception" pass that Franco Harris ultimately caught. Who was his intended target that many argue the ball bounced off of (which due to the rules at the time, would have made the pass incomplete once Harris touched the ball)?

47.     Ken Stabler was on the field for arguably the most "nicknamed" games or plays of the 70s era. Such plays as the "sea of hands" against the Dolphins, "holy roller" against the Chargers, as well as the "ghost to the post" against the Colts. What play was he known for in the "immaculate reception" game against the Steelers?
a.      Fumbled the ball to the Steelers 3 plays before the "immaculate reception".
b.      Threw an interception to Donnie Shell of the Steelers 3 plays before the "immaculate reception".
c.      Hit Cliff Branch on an 83-yard TD to give the Raiders the lead prior to the "immaculate reception".
d.      Ran 30 yards for a TD to give the Raiders the lead prior to the "immaculate reception".

48.     Bob Griese was the initial starting quarterback for the Miami Dolphins during their 1972 perfect undefeated season. However, he broke his leg and dislocated his ankle in the fifth game that year. What was the name of the backup quarterback who

filled in for him and won 10 straight games before Griese came back for the playoffs?

49.     In the Dallas Cowboys 1974 Thanksgiving Day game, Roger Staubach was knocked out of the game with a concussion. What quarterback famously came in for Staubach and led the Cowboys to a 24-23 come from behind win?

50.     These quarterbacks also wore jersey number 12: Jim Kelly, Andrew Luck, Joe Namath, and Rich Gannon. Of these four, only one has NOT thrown for at least 4,000 yards in a season. Which one?

51.     Oh, the terrible twos! Jamarcus Russell, Johnny Manziel and Zach Wilson were picked in the first round of their respective drafts (Russell going first overall). All three wore jersey number 2 and struggled mightily with many considering them as draft busts. Of the three which one threw for more yards and touchdowns in their NFL career?

52.     Johnny Manziel wasn't the only rookie quarterback who was picked in the first round by the Cleveland Browns, wore jersey #2 and also struggled in his career. Who was the other?

53.     Only Matt Ryan seems to have broken the curse of jersey number 2 when it comes to quarterbacks, at least so far. But Doug Flutie had an NFL career that many would call successful. While Flutie wore number 7 for much of his career with the Buffalo Bills and San Diego Chargers, he did wear jersey number 2 with the Chicago Bears and New England Patriots. What NFL team, and

in which round, was Heisman trophy winner Doug Flutie selected in the draft?

54.     How many seasons did Doug Flutie play in the NFL? Get this one correct and you are a true trivia All-Pro!

55.     Of the 19 available jersey numbers for quarterbacks (excluding double digit wearing quarterbacks such as John Hadl), only four have yet to be worn by the winning quarterback in the Super Bowl. What are those four jersey numbers?

56.     These 8s were (not so) great. Who were the last 2 quarterbacks to wear jersey number 8 for the Pittsburgh Steelers before Aaron Rodgers?

57.     The Fabulous Fives: During the first decade of the 2000s there were several solid quarterbacks in the NFC wearing jersey number 5 that you may have forgotten about. They include Jeff Garcia, Josh Freeman, Donovan McNabb and Kerry Collins. Of this contingent, who is the only one NOT to have thrown for 4,000 yards in a season?

58.     Of Jeff Garcia, Josh Freeman, Donovan McNabb and Kerry Collins, which of these quarterbacks went undrafted yet went on to be a 4-time Pro Bowler?

59.     Here are some fives who've struggled. In recent decades, unlike Jayden Daniels of the Commanders, and Joe Flacco of the Ravens, young quarterbacks wearing jersey number 5 have struggled. Anthony Richardson was the 4th overall pick of the

Indianapolis Colts in the 2023 draft. Trey Lance was the 3rd overall pick of the San Francisco Forty-Niners in the 2021 draft. Going back further, Blake Bortles was the 3rd overall pick of the Jacksonville Jaguars in the 2014 draft. Going back further still, Heath Shuler was the 3rd overall pick of the Washington Redskins in the 1994 draft. All of these quarterbacks struggled despite being selected early in the first round of their respective drafts. Of these four, which quarterback is the only one with a winning record as a starting quarterback?

60.  Of Anthony Richardson, Trey Lance, Blake Bortles and Heath Shuler, which quarterback has appeared in the least number of games in their NFL career?

61.  Here's a jersey number 5 one-hit wonder: What quarterback led his 1985 team to an 11-5 record and conference championship game appearance during his only NFL season?

62.  Who's #1? Name the only NFL MVP winner to wear jersey number 1.

63.  The Power of 11. Three players wearing jersey number 11 have gone on to win the Super Bowl MVP. Two are quarterbacks, the other is Julian Edelman. Who are the quarterbacks?

64.  Baker Mayfield, Mark Sanchez and Jay Cutler have all worn jersey number 6 in their NFL careers. Of these three, which has started in the most playoff games through the 2024 season?

65. Of the following jersey numbers, which has been worn by the most Hall of Famers?
a. 12
b. 14
c. 16
d. 18

*"Every game I've ever played, regardless if it was pre-season or Super Bowl, meant the same to me, and I laid it all on the line."*

*#4 Brett Favre*

# 4. All Shapes, Sizes and Abilities

Not all quarterbacks are the prototypical 6' 3" 225 pounds with a rifle right arm standing statuesque in the pocket. The following questions feature some lefties, some short kings, some NBA sized, some o-line sized and some who run as well as they pass. Here's to those that don't fit the mold.

## Lefties

66. Prior to Tua Tagovailoa taking the field in 2020, who was the NFL's last left-handed quarterback to play in the NFL?

67. Who was the first left-handed quarterback to be elected to the Pro Football Hall of Fame?

68. Who were the first two left-handed quarterbacks to face each other in the Super Bowl?

69. Who is the only left-handed quarterback drafted in the first round by the Raiders?

70. Name the college that each of the following left-handed quarterbacks played for prior to their NFL career.
a. David Humm
b. Bobby Douglass
c. Tim Tebow
d. Mark Brunell

71. What left-handed quarterback was AFC Offensive Rookie of the Year in 1976?

72. Who is the only left-handed UCLA Bruin quarterback drafted in the first round of the NFL draft?

73. Who was the first left-handed quarterback to win the Super Bowl?

74. Who are the only left-handed starting quarterbacks in the NFL going into the 2025 season?

75. Of lefties, Michael Vick, Boomer Esiason, Ken Stabler, and Mark Brunnell, which left-handed quarterback threw the most touchdown passes in his career?

## Does size matter?

76. Of Doug Flutie, Bryce Young, Johnny Manziel, and Russell Wilson, who is the tallest?

77. Who was the heaviest quarterback in the NFL?

78. What 2 quarterbacks listed at 6'7" have the Denver Broncos selected in their respective drafts?

79. Who is the tallest quarterback to have played in the NFL?

80. Of Colin Kaepernick, Trevor Lawrence, Nick Foles, and Joe Flacco, who is the shortest?

## They could run too!

81. Who holds the NFL regular season single game rushing record for a quarterback?

82. Who holds the NFL playoff single game rushing record for a quarterback?

83. Who is the only quarterback to rush for 1,000 yards in back-to-back seasons?

84. What quarterback is the single season rushing record holder?

85. In the Super Bowl era, what quarterback holds the record for most rushing touchdowns in a game?

*"Know why I smile so much out there? It's because I'm having so much fun."*

*#5 Donovan McNabb*

# 5. Heismans, MVPs and Other Awards

These questions focus on the best of the best, those award winners who earned the right to be recognized for their commitment to excellence. They've mastered the position and led their teams to prominence, some for more than a decade. Think you know who's been recognized as the best? Answer these questions and see.

86.  What two quarterbacks have won the Heisman Trophy as well as the NFL MVP Award?

87.  Archie Manning and son Eli Manning both finished third in the Heisman voting in their final year at Ole Miss. Who did each Manning lose out to in those years?

88.  Of Drew Brees, Joe Montana, Tom Brady and Peyton Manning, which quarterback has the most NFL MVP Awards?

89. Who has finished as the NFL MVP runner up the most times without ever winning the award?

90. Of John Elway, Jim Kelly, Boomer Esiason, and Dan Marino, which quarterback did not win the NFL MVP award?

91. Of Drew Brees, Joe Montana, Tom Brady and Peyton Manning, which quarterback has the fewest Pro Bowls to his credit?

92. Who is the only LSU quarterback to win the NFL MVP award?

93. Which of the following quarterbacks never won the NFL MVP award?
a. Boomer Esiason
b. Matt Ryan
c. Troy Aikman
d. Steve McNair

94. In the 1964 East West Shrine Game, these two future Super Bowl quarterbacks, who would soon share quarterback duties on the same NFL team, opposed each other, one playing for the West, the other playing for the East. Who were they?

95. Who was the first college walk-on to go on and win the Heisman Trophy?

96. There are two Heisman Trophy winning quarterbacks who went undrafted by the NFL. Who are they?

97. What four quarterbacks, who were their respective draft's overall number one pick, are in the Hall of Fame?

98. Who is the last Heisman Trophy Award winner to become a head coach in the NFL?

99. What two quarterbacks have unanimously earned NFL MVP honors?

100. Which Hall of Fame quarterback has thrown for more interceptions than Joe Montana and Troy Aikman combined?

101. How can it be? This quarterback was a Heisman Trophy winner, became the #1 overall pick in his draft, won two Super Bowls and was named Super Bowl MVP, yet as of this writing, he is not in the Hall of Fame. Who is he?

102. How many quarterbacks in the Super Bowl era are in the Hall of Fame without winning the Super Bowl?

103. What two undrafted free agent quarterbacks became NFL Hall of Famers?

104. What current NFL quarterback is the youngest Heisman Trophy winner in history?

*"When I woke up this morning, I was feeling pretty dangerous."*

*#6 Baker Mayfield*

## 6. Draft Selections

Many NFL football fans believe the season actually starts in April with the NFL draft. Each one has seen its share of pleasant surprises (think Tom Brady) as well as busts (think Jamarcus Russell). Here are some questions to test your quarterback draft knowledge.

105. Who are the 6 quarterbacks from the University of Oregon to be selected in the first round of the NFL draft since 1970?

106. Who was the only other quarterback picked in the first round of the 2007 NFL draft after the Raiders selected Jamarcus Russell?

107. Who were the two quarterbacks selected in the first round of the 2012 NFL Draft after Andrew Luck and Robert Griffin III?

108. Name the five quarterbacks from the 2020 NFL draft that started for their teams in the 2024 season.

109. In the 2012 draft the Washington Redskins surprised many by taking 2 quarterbacks. Robert Griffin III was selected #2 overall. Who was the other quarterback they selected and in what round?

110. In the 2015 NFL draft the top overall pick as well as the second pick in the draft were quarterbacks. These two quarterbacks were both Heisman Trophy winners. Who are they?

111. Of Eli Manning, Phillip Rivers and Ben Roethlisberger, the top 3 quarterbacks selected in the 2004 draft, who had the most career touchdown passes?

112. Brock Purdy of the San Francisco Forty-Niners is not the only quarterback selected last in the draft as Mr. Irrelevant. Who are the other two?

113. In the 2003 NFL draft Eli Manning, Philip Rivers and Ben Roethlisberger were all selected in the first round. Who was the 4th quarterback also selected in the first round of that draft?

114. What two University of Houston quarterbacks were selected in the 1990 and 1992 NFL drafts in the first round?

115. In the 1994 NFL draft the Indianapolis Colts were on the clock with the 5th overall pick. They selected linebacker Trev Alberts of Nebraska leading to a career defining meltdown by

ESPN draft analyst Mel Kiper, Jr. Kiper lambasted the Colts saying they should have taken this quarterback instead. Who is he?

116.   What three quarterbacks, who were their respective draft's overall number one pick, won NFL Offensive Rookie of the Year honors?

117.   Many thought that Shedeur Sanders would be selected in the first round of the 2025 NFL draft. The New Orleans Saints, with Derek Carr's future uncertain, were reportedly interested. However, the Saints chose offensive tackle Kelvin Banks with their first-round pick instead. Who was the last quarterback the Saints drafted in the first round?

118.   Brett Favre was a second-round pick of the Atlanta Falcons in the 1991 NFL draft. Who were the two quarterbacks that were drafted ahead of him?

119.   Jim Kelly, a hero in Buffalo, was selected in the 1983 NFL draft by the Bills with the 14th pick of the first round. However, he was not the first player selected by the Bills. Who did the Bills select with the 12th pick of the first round that year?

120.   Jim Kelly, although selected in the first round by the Buffalo Bills in the 1983 draft, chose to start his career in the USFL. Which team did he play for while ultimately winning the USFL MVP Award?

121.   Future Hall of Famer Patrick Mahomes was selected by the Kansas City Chiefs in the first round of the 2017 NFL draft (10th

overall). Who was the last quarterback to be taken in the first round by the Chiefs prior to Mahomes?

122.  Which quarterback was chosen highest in their respective drafts?
a.  Dan Marino
b.  Lamar Jackson
c.  Drew Brees
d.  Aaron Rodgers

123.  Who are the 6 quarterbacks that were selected before Tom Brady in the 2000 NFL draft?

124.  How many times did the Colts select a quarterback with the #1 overall pick in the NFL draft? Can you name them?

125.  2025 first overall draft pick Cam Ward was a zero-star recruit coming out of high school. Where did he play his freshman year in college?

126.  Of 2025 draftees Cam Ward, Jaxson Dart, Dillon Gabriel, and Shedeur Sanders, which quarterback threw for the most yards in their college career?

127.  Two college universities can claim that they produced 3 quarterbacks who were their draft's number one overall selection. Can you name the two schools as well as the 3 quarterbacks from each that were the overall top pick of their draft? Hint: All 6 of these players were NFL starters.

128. Who was the last USC quarterback before Caleb Williams to be the NFL's number one overall draft selection?

*"I don't think the NFL has ever seen the likes of me, a quarterback who moves the way I do and throws the way I do. I'm not saying that with arrogance or anything. That is just how I feel."*

*#7 Michael Vick*

# 7. Post Season Performances

The games' brightest stars featured on the biggest stage! How well do you know the quarterbacks that have led their teams to the playoffs, the Super Bowl and the Lombardi Trophy? We're about to find out!

129. True or False. John Elway has thrown for more interceptions than touchdowns in the 5 Super Bowls that he has played in.

130. Who are the 3 teams that beat John Elway in the Super Bowl?

131. What 2 quarterbacks both threw for over 400 yards in the 1982 AFC Divisional Playoff between the San Diego Chargers and Miami Dolphins, a game that many consider the greatest of all time

(NOTE: This is the game where Kellen Winslow had to be helped off the field)?

132. Who were the starting quarterbacks in the "Harbaugh Bowl" (AKA, "Bro Bowl", "Super Baugh", "Har Bowl") which pitted John Harbaugh's Baltimore Ravens against Jim Harbaugh's San Francisco Forty-Niners in Super Bowl XLVII?

133. Of the following quarterbacks, which was never a Super Bowl MVP: Jim Plunkett, Len Dawson, Bob Griese, or Doug Williams?

134. What college is represented by the most quarterbacks who have started in a Super Bowl?

135. Who are the 3 Notre Dame quarterbacks that have led their team to a Super Bowl?

136. Who are the 3 Purdue quarterbacks that have led their team to a Super Bowl?

137. Which of the following universities has not had at least 2 quarterbacks start in the Super Bowl?
a. Washington State
b. Ohio State
c. Boston College
d. Maryland

138. Who is the first starting quarterback to appear in the Super Bowl with more than one franchise?

139.   Who is the only quarterback to lead his team to 4 straight Super Bowls?

140.   Who was the quarterback to lead the Los Angeles Rams to their first Super Bowl?

141.   Who are the two quarterbacks to lead the Carolina Panthers to the Super Bowl?

142.   Who was the quarterback to lead the San Diego Chargers to their first Super Bowl?

143.   Who was the quarterback to lead the Dallas Cowboys to their first Super Bowl?

144.   Who is the first starting quarterback to win the Super Bowl with 2 different teams?

145.   Who is the first starting quarterback to play in 4 Super Bowls with 2 different teams each?

146.   Who is the only starting quarterback to play in 4 Super Bowls under 4 different head coaches?

147. Who is the only quarterback to throw for 6 touchdowns in a Super Bowl?

148. What NFL quarterback has the most career passing yards without winning a Super Bowl?

149. What was the score of the "Immaculate Reception" game?

150. The Washington Redskins (now Commanders) won 3 Super Bowls under head coach Joe Gibbs with 3 different starting quarterbacks. Who were those quarterbacks?

151. Who are the quarterbacks NOT named Tom Brady that have started a Super Bowl game for the New England Patriots.

152. How many quarterbacks have started for the Philadelphia Eagles in the Super Bowl?

153. Dan Marino, Jim Kelly, Dan Fouts, Warren Moon, and Phillip Rivers are all legendary quarterbacks who have not won the Super Bowl. Which of these greats has the best playoff record?

154. Who holds the NFL record for consecutive regular season games with a touchdown pass?

155.   What NFL quarterback holds the record for most passing yards and touchdown passes in a Rose Bowl game?

156.   What NFL quarterback holds the record for most passing yards and touchdown passes in a College Football Playoff National Championship game?

*"The principle is competing against yourself. It's about self-improvement, about being better than you were the day before."*

*#8 Steve Young*

## 8. Statistically Speaking

While stats aren't as important as Super Bowl championships, it's still fun to use them to compare quarterbacks and their careers. These questions are harder than most. Think you're ready? Let's go!

157. Going into the 2025 season, of Patrick Mahomes, Josh Allen, Joe Burrow and Lamar Jackson, which quarterback has not thrown for at least 40 touchdowns in a season?

158. Going into the 2025 season, of Joe Burrow, Josh Allen, Lamar Jackson, or Justin Herbert, which quarterback has the highest career QB rating?

159. What 2 opposing quarterbacks combined to throw for the most passing yards in a single game in NFL history?

160. What 2 opposing quarterbacks combined to throw for the most touchdowns in a single game in NFL history?

161. What quarterback holds the NFL record for most pass attempts in a single game?

162. Rank order these quarterbacks from highest career playoff passer rating to lowest career playoff passer rating: Drew Brees, Joe Montana, Tom Brady and Peyton Manning.

163. What NFL quarterback is the career leader in 4th quarter comebacks?

164. What NFL quarterback is the career leader in game winning drives?

165. What 3 quarterbacks share the single game record for being sacked?

166. What quarterback threw the most interceptions in a single season in the Super Bowl era?

167. What quarterback has led the NFL in passes intercepted the highest number of times?

168. What NFL quarterback holds the record for consecutive pass attempts thrown without an interception?

169. Of the following QBs, which threw for more yards in their NFL career?
a. Russell Wilson
b. Dan Marino
c. Matt Ryan
d. John Elway

170. Of the quarterbacks below, which is the only one with a winning record during the regular season?
a. Warren Moon
b. Joe Namath
c. Boomer Esiason
d. Eli Manning

171. Who are the only two quarterbacks to have thrown for more than 500 yards in a playoff game in the Super Bowl era?

172. What NFL quarterback has thrown for 5,000 yards with two different teams?

173. Rank order these quarterbacks from most career passing yards to fewest career passing yards.
a. Kerry Collins
b. Jay Cutler
c. Ryan Tannehill
d. Phil Simms

174. This quarterback has thrown for more career touchdowns than Jim Kelly, Steve Young, and Joe Namath combined. Who is he?

## PRO FOOTBALL TRIVIA - QUARTERBACKS

175. Which of the quarterbacks below has the following career statistics: 71,838 yards passing, 508 touchdowns, 336 interceptions, and 28 4th quarter comebacks?
a.  Dan Marino
b.  John Elway
c.  Joe Montana
d.  Brett Favre

176. Of the NFL quarterbacks on a 2025 Roster, which one has the most 4th quarter comebacks in their career?

177. Of the following quarterbacks, which has the most game winning drives?
a.  Joe Flacco
b.  Kurt Cousins
c.  Aaron Rodgers
d.  Russell Wilson

178. In the Super Bowl era, what quarterback is the career passing yards per attempt leader?

179. Which NFL quarterback has five 5,000 yard passing seasons?

180. Which NFL quarterback has thrown for more than 4,000 yards for 12 consecutive seasons?

181. What NFL quarterback holds the record for most fumble recoveries in a season?

182. Which of the following quarterbacks has NOT thrown for 50 touchdowns in a single NFL season?
a. Drew Brees
b. Patrick Mahomes
c. Tom Brady
d. Peyton Manning

183. Through the 2024 NFL season, what quarterback has been sacked the most in his career?

*"I'm a very modest person. But I'm also extremely confident. And if you put me in the situation or in the moment, I'm gonna have some swagger, I'm gonna have some cockiness."*

#9 Drew Brees

## 9. "Name" That Quarterback

Every quarterback has a name they're known by. Some, like Joe and Steve, are more common than others, like Dak and C.J. Grouping quarterbacks with like names and then creating trivia questions around them? Priceless!

184.  Of A.J. McCarron, C.J. Beathard, C.J. Stroud, and EJ Manuel, which is named after his father, a successful music songwriter?

185.  What is Dak Prescott's full name?

186.  What is C.J. Stroud's full name?

187.  With what team did each of these Matt's end their NFL career?

a. Matt Leinhart
b. Matt Schaub
c. Matt Hasselback
d. Matt Cassel
e. Matt Ryan

188. Speaking of Matts, how many times did Matt Ryan throw for at least 4,000 yards?

189. Of all the NFL quarterbacks in modern history with the first name of Steve, which has the most career regular season passing yards?

190. Not your average Joes. Rank order these quarterbacks named Joe from most career passing yards to fewest career passing yards.
a. Joe Flacco
b. Joe Kapp
c. Joe Ferguson
d. Joe Theisman

191. Who threw for more career passing yards, Billy Joe Tolliver or Billy Joe Hobert?

192. Rank order the following "Drews" from highest NFL career yards per pass completion to lowest career yards per pass completion.
a. Drew Bledsoe
b. Drew Stanton
c. Drew Lock
d. Drew Brees

193. Of Chris Weinke, Chris Miller, Chris Chandler, and Chris Simms, which quarterback threw for the most yards during their rookie season?

194. Of Jeff Hostetler, Jeff Blake, Jeff Garcia, and Jeff George, which quarterback never made the Pro Bowl?

195. Who are the 4 quarterbacks with the first name Joe who have won a Super Bowl?

196. Of Tommy Kramer, Tommy Maddox and Tommy DeVito, which quarterback has not played for the New York Giants?

197. Of Bobby Hoying, Bobby Douglass, and Bobby Hebert, which quarterback is the only one to make the Pro Bowl?

198. Of Billy Kilmer, Tommy Kramer, Jimmy Garoppolo, and Johnny Unitas, which quarterback never passed for at least 3,000 yards in a season?

199. Of Steve Spurrier, Steve Bartkowski, Steve DeBerg, and Steve Bono, which quarterback did not play for the San Francisco Forty-Niners?

200. Who are the 3 starting quarterbacks named Joe that lost in the Super Bowl?

201. Of Vince Ferragamo, Vince Young, and Vince Evans, which quarterback threw for the most career yards and touchdowns?

*"I went through that phase where I wanted to almost be different than my brother. Just kind of argued a little louder or if there was a curfew, I always came in a little later than I was supposed to. If it was set for 12, I would come in at 12:45. I would test the limits a little. There was no real reason and I grew out of it eventually.*

#10 Eli Manning

## 10. One For Each Team

With the following questions we feature every team in the NFL. How well do you know the quarterback history of your favorite team?

202. Who was the last quarterback to lead the Carolina Panthers to a playoff victory?

203. In between Michael Vick's last season with the Atlanta Falcons (2006) and Matt Flynn's first (2008), what 3 quarterbacks started games during the 2007 season?

204. Of Phil Simms, Kurt Warner, Daniel Jones and Eli Manning, which New York Giant quarterback had the highest completion percentage while with the team?

205. What was the New Orleans Saints record in 2005, the year before Drew Brees became their quarterback?

206. Who is the only quarterback to play for the Houston Oilers, Tennessee Oilers, and Tennessee Titans?

207. Who was the first Houston Texans quarterback to win a playoff game?

208. What Jacksonville Jaguar quarterback has won the most playoff games for the franchise?

209. Of Ryan Fitzpatrick, Chad Pennington, Jay Fiedler, and Chad Henne, which Miami Dolphins quarterback guided the team to the most wins as a starter?

210. In 2011 Indianapolis Colts quarterback Peyton Manning sat out the entire season, his last as a Colt, due to neck surgery. Who was the Colts season opening starter at quarterback that year? Hint: It wasn't Andrew Luck. Luck wouldn't be drafted until the following year.

211. On Thanksgiving Day of 2012 New York Jets quarterback Mark Sanchez ran into the backside of a lineman causing what has come to be known as the "Butt Fumble". What is the name of the lineman that Sanchez ran into?

212. The Washington Redskins won 3 Super Bowls with 3 different quarterbacks under head coach Joe Gibbs. Of the 3 quarterbacks, which one did not win Super Bowl MVP?

213. Of Kevin Kolb, Randall Cunningham, Donovan McNabb and Carson Wentz, which Philadelphia Eagles quarterback threw for the most touchdowns as a rookie?

214. Who was the last Buffalo Bills quarterback before Josh Allen to make the Pro Bowl?

215. Who was the last New England Patriot quarterback to make the Pro Bowl as a rookie before Drake Maye did it in 2024?

216. Who is the Pro Bowl quarterback who led the Pittsburgh Steelers to an appearance in Super Bowl XXX only to contribute to the Cowboys' Cornerback Larry Brown being voted game MVP?

217. Of Jim Harbaugh, Kyle Boller, Trent Dilfer, and Tony Banks, which quarterback started more games for the Baltimore Ravens?

218. Sandwiched in between the John Elway and Peyton Manning eras for the Denver Broncos are quarterbacks Brian Griese, Jake Plummer, Jay Cutler, and Kyle Orton. Of these quarterbacks, who started more games for the Broncos?

219. Who holds the Kansas City Chiefs record for most touchdown passes by a rookie? HINT: He also holds the Chiefs record for most interceptions thrown by a rookie.

220. Who is the last ever draft pick by the Raiders Al Davis who would play both quarterback and receiver with the team before becoming a full-time receiver with the Browns, Jets, Redskins, and Bills.

221. Of Teddy Bridgewater, Randall Cunningham, Christian Ponder, and Rich Gannon, who has thrown for more yards while in a Minnesota Vikings uniform?

222. Who is the Chicago Bears career passing yardage leader? HINT: He has passed for more yards than Jim McMahon and Jim Harbaugh combined.

223. What Arizona Cardinals quarterback, who is in their ring of honor, won the Walter Payton Man of the Year as well as being voted the starting Pro Bowl quarterback that same year?

224. Of Jeff George, Jeff Garcia, Jeff Komlo and Jon Kitna, which quarterback never played for the Detroit Lions.

225. Who are the 3 Green Bay Packer quarterbacks not named Aaron Rodgers or Brett Favre to throw for at least 400 yards in a game?

226. Who are the two quarterbacks that the Cincinnati Bengals have chosen with the #1 overall pick in their respective drafts?

227. Who are the two quarterbacks that the Cincinnati Bengals have chosen with the #3 overall pick in their respective drafts?

228. Who was the first Tampa Bay Buccaneer quarterback to go to the Pro Bowl?

229. Who are the 4 Detroit Lions quarterbacks to throw for 4,000 yards in a season?

230. Which of the following Kansas City Chief quarterbacks has not thrown for 4,000 yards in a season?

a. Trent Green
b. Alex Smith
c. Joe Montana
d. Elvis Grbac

231. Of the following San Francisco Forty-Niner quarterbacks not named Montana or Young, who has thrown for more yards and touchdowns in their Forty-Niner career: Alex Smith, Jeff Garcia, or Jimmy Garopollo?

232. Rank order these Dallas Cowboy quarterbacks from most career passing yards to fewest career passing yards.
a. Danny White
b. Roger Staubach
c. Tony Romo
d. Troy Aikman

233. Of Baker Mayfield, Bernie Kosar, Vinny Testaverde and Brian Sipe, who is the only one that did not have a winning record when quarterbacking the Cleveland Browns?

234. Who was San Francisco Forty-Niner Joe Montana's initial intended receiver, i.e., first option, when he instead threw to Dwight Clark for "The Catch" in a 1982 playoff game against the Dallas Cowboys?

235. Who is the Rams all-time passing yards leader?

236. Who was the Seattle Seahawks starting quarterback the season after Matt Hasselbeck's final with the team and the year before Russell Wilson's first?

*"Of course, it looks bad when you're not executing. When things go bad, it's not going to look good."*

*#11 Phil Simms*

## 11. Bonus Baby!

Want some more? We've got more! These are extra tough so grit your teeth and let's go!

237. Nothing against Scott Bruner and Matt Nagy, but we are the two best quarterbacks to play at the University of Delaware. We've both quarterbacked 17 years in the NFL as well as thrown for 4,000 yards in a season. One of us has won the NFL MVP award while the other has won the Super Bowl MVP award. Who are we?

238. Who was the Green Bay Packer quarterback that Brett Favre replaced?

239. These Super Bowl winning quarterbacks attended the same Texas high school albeit 8 years apart. Who are they?

240. What Super Bowl winning quarterback attended the same high school as Barry Bonds, albeit about 10 years apart?

241. How many NFL teams has Ryan Fitzpatrick played for?

242. For what university did Ryan Fitzpatrick play his collegiate football?

243. Jim Kelly, while quarterbacking the Houston Gamblers of the USFL, ran the offense known as the "Run and Shoot", a scheme devised by the legendary Mouse Davis. What was the nickname of the offense he ran with the Buffalo Bills?

244. Who is the first quarterback to have a passing touchdown, rushing touchdown and receiving touchdown all in the same game?

245. Who are the 3 quarterbacks who each had a receiving touchdown during the 2024 NFL season?

246. What two quarterbacks have thrown for at least one touchdown pass for 7 different NFL franchises?

247. What is the only team that Ryan Fitzpatrick played for where he did not throw a touchdown or interception?

248. What NFL head coach played quarterback in an NFL game as a replacement player for the Chicago Bears (known as the "Spare Bears") during the NFL players strike in 1987?

249. What four 2025 NFL head coaches played at least one down of quarterback in a regular season NFL game?

250. Brett Favre holds an interesting distinction that no one else can claim. What happened on his very first NFL pass attempt?

251. What is the real name of Boomer Esiason who led the Cincinnati Bengals to Super Bowl XXIII, a loss to the San Francisco Forty-Niners?

252. Troy Aikman was a standout collegiate player prior to being the #1 overall pick in the 1989 draft by the Dallas Cowboys. His senior year at UCLA he was not named First Team All Pac 12. Another quarterback, who would go on to a solid NFC career, was. That player also finished ahead of Aikman in the 1988 Heisman Trophy voting. Who was he?

253. BYU has had plenty of quarterbacks go on to play in the NFL including Steve Young, Jim McMahon, and Marc Wilson. All three had winning NFL records as NFL starters. Which of the 3 had the highest yards per completion average during their NFL career?

254. Who was the first quarterback ever to be ejected from an NFL game?

255. Who was the second quarterback ever to be ejected from an NFL game?

256. Pat yourself on the back if you get this one. Baker Mayfield credits his 5-game stint with the Los Angeles Rams after being

released by the Carolina Panthers with rejuvenating his career. He was picked up by the Rams on December 6, 2022 after starter Matthew Stafford was injured. With only two days to learn the playbook it was doubtful that coach Sean McVay would play Mayfield. The Rams started Stafford's backup but benched him after the first offensive series and inserted Mayfield who would go on and help the Rams win the game beating the Raiders. Who was the backup quarterback who got benched?

257. True or False, Tom Brady had more career playoff wins than Peyton Manning, Eli Manning and Troy Aikman combined.

258. What are the first names of the two Kramers that played quarterback primarily for NFC Central teams in the 80s and 90s?

259. In the 1984 season Dan Marino threw for 5,084 yards, 48 yards and 17 interceptions. Who were his two favorite wide receivers who accounted for 144 receptions and 2,695 yards between them?

260. Who is the Minnesota Vikings career passing yardage leader?

261. What wide receiver had 8 pass attempts completing 4 for 106 yards, 2 touchdowns and 1 interception while playing for the Minnesota Vikings?

262. What 3 NFL quarterbacks each threw for 5,000 yards in a season and were NOT on the Pro Bowl roster for their 5,000-yard year?

*"To be successful at anything, the truth is you don't have to be special. You just have to be what most people aren't: consistent, determined, and willing to work for it. No shortcuts."*

#12 Tom Brady

## 12. But Wait, There's More, A Lot More!

We're not done yet. Here's more quarterback trivia questions to impress your buddies with.

263. What player is the career rushing leader for a quarterback?

264. What 4 quarterbacks have each rushed for more yards in their career than Hall of Fame running back Gayle Sayers?

265. According to Public.com, which of the following is the most expensive football card featuring a quarterback?
    a. 1957 Topps Bart Starr Rookie Card #119
    b. 2000 SP Authentic Tom Brady Rookie Card #118
    c. 2017 National Treasures NFL Shield Patrick Mahomes Autographed Rookie Card #161

266.	Stanford has churned out some great quarterbacks over the years including Andrew Luck, Jim Plunkett, John Brodie and of course, John Elway. Which of these four has never won a regular season MVP or Super Bowl MVP?

267.	Other Stanford quarterbacks who played in the NFL include Davis Mills (who as of this writing is still playing), Turk Schonert, Steve Dils, and Steve Stenstrom. Of these four, which quarterback has had the longest NFL career?

268.	Kordell Stewart, Hines Ward and Antwaan Randle-El each played multiple positions in college, including quarterback, before playing for the Pittsburgh Steelers in the NFL. Of the three, Stewart, AKA "Slash", is the only one to start at QB in the NFL. For what two teams did Stewart play for besides the Steelers?

269.	Can you name the 3 Heisman Trophy quarterbacks who played their collegiate career at the University of Florida?

270.	Speaking of Florida quarterbacks, Tim Tebow played only two years for the Denver Broncos after they selected him with the 25th pick in the first round of the 2010 NFL draft. He was traded to the New York Jets who released him after one season. Who are the 3 teams that would go on to sign Tebow only to release him before he played another regular season game?

271.	Can you name the 4 Heisman Trophy quarterbacks who played their collegiate career at the University of Oklahoma, 3 of which went on to play in the NFL.

272.	Who is the only Ohio State University quarterback to win the Heisman Trophy and go on to play in the NFL?

273. Cincinnati Bengals quarterback Joe Burrow began his college career at Ohio State University. He sat for his first two seasons behind starter J.T. Barrett. Going into the next season he believed he would sit yet again, this time behind this quarterback who would go on to become a first round NFL draft choice. Who was that quarterback that prompted Burrow to transfer to LSU?

274. What two University of Miami quarterbacks won the Heisman trophy and were selected in the NFL draft.

275. In 2013 Peyton Manning, playing for the Denver Broncos, threw 55 touchdown passes, an NFL record. How many of those touchdown passes were to running backs?

276. Of Tom Brady, Peyton Manning, Brett Favre and Drew Brees, which quarterback or quarterbacks (you can choose more than one) has beaten all 32 NFL teams?

277. Through the 2024 season Aaron Rodgers has thrown for more than 80,000 regular season yards. He has surpassed the 4,000-yard benchmark in 10 of his 20 seasons. In how many seasons has he thrown 10 or more interceptions?

278. Of Tom Brady, Peyton Manning, Aaron Rogers, and Drew Brees, which quarterback has thrown more than 20 interceptions in a season twice in their career?

279. Josh Allen of the Buffalo Bills is the 2nd player to win NFL MVP while wearing jersey number 17. Who was the first to wear that number and win league MVP?

280. Who was the last player to wear jersey number 12 for the New England Patriots before Tom Brady?

281. Who was the last player to wear jersey number 12 for the Green Bay Packers before Aaron Rodgers?

282. True or False, Steve Young, Warren Moon, Dan Marino and Michael Vick, all have the same average yards per pass completion rate for their career.

283. Another quarterback you may have forgotten about is Ken Anderson. Anderson played 16 years in the NFL, all for the Cincinnati Bengals. He was NFL MVP in 1981 the year he led the Bengals to their first Super Bowl. Two questions: Where did he play his college ball, and in the NFL, what jersey number did he wear?

284. What 3 NFL quarterbacks threw for 5,000 yards during the 2011 season?

285. The first round of the 1999 NFL Draft produced Hall of Fame Running Back Edgerrin James (pick #4 of the Colts), and Defensive Back Champ Bailey (pick #7 of the Washington Redskins). Five quarterbacks were selected within the first 12 picks of that draft. How many of those quarterbacks can you name?

286. What quarterback who has appeared in at least 200 games has the lowest win percentage as a starting quarterback?

287. While Norm Van Brocklin holds the NFL single game passing yards record (554 yards), what two quarterbacks of the Super Bowl era share 2nd place on that list?

288. This one is tricky: What Purdue quarterback was taken with the 3rd overall pick in the 1986 draft by the Houston Oilers?

289. As a follow up to that question, who is the other Purdue quarterback that was taken with the 3rd overall pick in his draft 16 years earlier? Hint: He was selected by the Cleveland Browns.

290. Who are the four quarterbacks to start for two different teams in the Super Bowl?

291. Jalen Hurts, Tua Tagovailoa, A.J. McCarron, Bryce Young, Joe Namath, and Mac Jones all played in the NFL after playing at Alabama. Which of these quarterbacks threw for the most yards for the Crimson Tide?

292. What two former NFL quarterbacks went on to become United States Congressmen?

293. Brigham Young University has had some legendary college quarterbacks over the years. Some of them are well known such as Jim McMahon, Steve Young, and Ty Detmer. Others with excellent careers there include John Beck, Max Hall, Steve Sarkisian, and Steve Walsh. Of these last four, which one never played a down in the NFL?

294. Of Dan Pastorini, George Blanda, Ryan Tannehill, and Vince Young, which quarterback is not in the top 5 of the

Tennessee Titans/Houston Oilers career passing yardage leaders for that franchise?

295. Of legendary Green Bay Packer quarterbacks, Brett Favre, Aaron Rodgers, and Bart Starr, which had the highest win percentage of the games they started for the Packers?

296. Who was the last NFL quarterback to throw 7 interceptions in one game?

297. Who is the only quarterback to throw 6 interceptions in 3 different games in the Super Bowl era?

298. What punter once threw 6 interceptions in a game as a starting NFL quarterback?

299. Tom Brady has played every NFL team at least once. What three teams have never beaten Tom Brady?

300. What is the only NFL team that has a winning record against Tom Brady when including the playoffs?

# ANSWERS

# Answers - Who Am I?

1. Marcus Mariota. Mariota won the Heisman Trophy in 2014 after a strong career at Oregon. He was selected #2 overall by the Tennessee Titans in the 2015 draft behind Jameis Winston. On January 6, 2018, in his first playoff appearance against the Kansas City Chiefs in the Wild Card round, Mariota caught his own pass that was deflected by Darelle Revis for a 6-yard touchdown. The Titans would come back from a 21-3 deficit to win the game 22-21.

2. Brad Johnson. Johnson was drafted by the Minnesota Vikings in the 1992 draft. He played for the Vikings and Redskins before landing in Tampa to play for the Buccaneers (he would later go back to Minnesota before ending his career in Dallas). He won Super Bowl XXXVII with the Buccaneers on January 26, 2003 when they defeated the Oakland Raiders 48-21. On October 12, 1997, in a game against the Carolina Panthers, Johnson caught his

own deflected pass and ran it into the end zone. It goes down as a 3-yard pass, however, he caught the deflected ball on the 8 before faking out a defender and diving in for the score.

3.     Doug Pederson. Pederson played for Miami, Green Bay, Philadelphia and Cleveland before returning to Green Bay. He was a backup to Brett Farve a majority of his career. He is now best known as the coach of the Philadelphia Eagles who called for the "Philly, Philly" or "Philly Special" on 4th down in Super Bowl LII in 2018, a 41-33 victory over the New England Patriots.

4.     Joe Montana. Montana was 1986 NFL Comeback Player of the Year after injuring his back the previous season. He of course won 2 NFL MVPs and 3 Super Bowl MVPs. He famously led Notre Dame to a thrilling come from behind victory in the 1979 Cotton Bowl after being down 34-12 late in the third quarter. That game is known as the "Chicken Soup Bowl" as Montana, suffering from mild hypothermia, was fed chicken soup at halftime of the game in addition to an IV. Notre Dame won the game 35-34. He also led the Forty-Niners from the brink of defeat in Super Bowl XXII in 1989. Trailing the Bengals 16–13 with 3:20 left in the game, the Forty-Niners were on their own 8-yard line needing at least a field goal to tie. On this drive Montana connected on 8 of 9 passes tossing the game-winning touchdown pass to receiver John Taylor with 34 ticks left on the clock. He was out all of 1991 and most of 1992 after injuring his elbow. With Steve Young now established as the Forty-Niner starter, Montana signs with the Chiefs and soon leads them to their first AFC Championship game

since 1970. In that game they lost to Jim Kelly and the Buffalo Bills, at Buffalo 30-13.


5.     David Carr. Carr is the older brother of Derek Carr. Both went to Fresno State. Derek, by the way, threw for 536 yards against San Diego State in a 2012 game. David Carr was selected #1 overall by the expansion Houston Texans team in the 2002 draft. He was Eli Manning's backup for Super Bowl XLVI in 2012 where the New York Giants defeated the New England Patriots 21-17.


6.     Steve Grogan. Grogan quarterbacked the New England Patriots after being selected in the 1975 draft. On January 26, 1986 Grogan was 17-30 and 177 yards with one TD against the vaunted Chicago Bears defense. The Bears, with what many believe to be the best defense in the history of the NFL, won the game 46-10 sacking Grogan 4 times and causing him to throw 2 interceptions. The neck roll Grogan wore was a result of a herniated disc and pinched nerve.


7.     Drew Bledsoe. Bledsoe was taken #1 overall by the New England Patriots in the 1993 draft out of Washington State University. After getting injured in a game against the Jets, the Patriots inserted Tom Brady who, much like baseball's Lou Gehrig, never relinquished the job.

8.     Jason Campbell. The Washington Redskins moved up in the draft to select Campbell in 2005 after his strong 4-year collegiate career at Auburn. After the Redskins, Campbell played for the Raiders, Bears, Browns and Bengals. He threw for 16,771 yards with 87 touchdowns and 60 interceptions over his 10 NFL seasons.

9.     Oliver Luck, father of Andrew Luck. Oliver Luck was selected with the 44th pick of the 1982 NFL draft by the Houston Oilers. He was the third quarterback taken after Art Schlichter and Jim McMahon (no relation to Vince McMahon).

10.    Drew Brees. Brees was selected with the 1st selection in the second round of the 2001 draft, 32nd overall, by the San Diego Chargers.

11.    Mac Jones. Jones, the 15th overall pick of the 2021 draft, was a redshirt freshman when Tua Tagovailoa was a sophomore and Jalen Hurts was a junior in the quarterback room at Alabama. After a great rookie season for the New England Patriots (he was second to Ja'Marr Chase in the Offensive Rookie of the Year voting), Jones' performance declined while Tua found success in Miami and Hurts, Philadelphia's second round pick in the 2020 draft, went on to win the 2025 Super Bowl.

12.    Russell Wilson. Wilson was chosen with the 75th pick of the 2012 NFL draft. He made the Pro Bowl as a rookie while

guiding the Seattle Seahawks to a 11-5 record before going 1-1 in the playoffs. With 25 seconds remaining in Super Bowl XLIX in 2015, the Seahawks had 2nd down on the Patriots' 1 yard line down 28-24. Rather than give the ball to Marshawn Lynch, Wilson threw a quick slant pass to Ricardo Lockette but was picked off by the Patriots' Malcolm Butler.

13.     Geno Smith. Smith led the Seahawks to a 10-7 record, narrowly missing the playoffs. Baker Mayfield, Jared Goff and Sam Darnold were voted to the Pro Bowl over Smith. Prior to the 2025 season the Seahawks traded Smith to the Las Vegas Raiders for a 3rd round draft pick.

14.     Dave Kreig. Kreig attended Milton College which closed its doors in 1982 due to financial difficulties. He played 12 seasons with the Seahawks where he is a member of their Ring of Honor. On November 11, 1990 the Seahawks played Derrick Thomas and the Chiefs at Arrowhead. On the last play of the game, Kreig eluded yet another sack and hit Paul Skansi for the win.

15.     Jim Plunkett. Plunket won the 1970 Heisman Trophy and was selected #1 overall by the Patriots in 1971. He quarterbacked the Oakland Raiders to victory over the Philadelphia Eagles 27-10 in Super Bowl XV in 1981 and was named Super Bowl MVP.

16.     Tommy Maddox. Maddox was selected in the first round as the heir apparent to John Elway even though he only played two

years at UCLA. His last season at UCLA he threw for 2,505 yards, 16 touchdowns and 15 interceptions. His entire UCLA career saw him throw for 33 touchdowns and 29 interceptions while completing less than 60% of his passes.

17.    David Woodley. Woodley was the Miami Dolphins team MVP as a rookie in 1980. By the 1982 season he had garnered the majority of the playing time although Don Strock also saw plenty of action. Woodley started for the Dolphins in Super Bowl XVII in 1983 and completed a touchdown pass to Jimmy Cefalo early on. It wasn't enough as Joe Theisman led Washington to victory. The next season, Don Shula replaced Woodley with rookie Dan Marino during the 5th game of the season. Woodley, who replaced Hall of Famer Bob Griese, went on to play two seasons for the Pittsburgh Steelers before retiring.

18.    Joe Pisarcik. On November 19, 1978, Pisarcik, with his New York Giants team ahead of the Philadelphia Eagles 17-12 with under 30 seconds left to play, bobbled the snap, then turned to hand the ball off to Larry Csonka, fumbling in the process. Herman Edwards picked up the loose ball and ran into the end zone giving the Eagles, who had no time outs, the win which became known as "The Miracle at the Meadowlands".

19.    Jay Schroeder. Schroeder was traded by the Redskins to the Raiders for tackle Jim Lachey who would go on to play several Pro Bowl seasons for Washington. Schroeder would eventually be replaced, first by Todd Marinovich and then by Jeff Hostetler.

20.     Chris Chandler. Chandler, a University of Washington product, was selected by the Indianapolis Colts in the third round with the 76th pick of the 1988 draft.

## *Answers - Two Truths and a Lie*

21. The correct answer is B. Lomax was actually the second quarterback selected in the 1981 draft. Rich Campbell of Cal was selected by the Green Bay Packers with the #6 overall pick that year. Lomax would go on to play for the St. Louis and Phoenix Cardinals from 1981-1988 passing for 22,721 yards, 136 touchdowns and 90 interceptions. He played his college ball at Portland State University.

22. The correct answer is C. Hostetler, who played for the Giants, Raiders and Redskins, made the Pro Bowl only once, in 1994 with the Raiders.

23. The correct answer is B. Cunningham did not fumble 3 times in the "Fog Bowl" but instead threw 3 interceptions and no touchdowns. He was 27-54 for 407 yards. The Bears won the game 20-12.

24. The correct answer is B. In his rookie year, Montana had 3 rushing attempts for 22 yards. He did have a 53-yard touchdown run in a 1984 playoff game however.

25. The correct answer is C. Through the 2024 season Tony Romo is the career leader for the Cowboys in game winning drives and 4th quarter comebacks with 29 and 24 respectively.

26. The correct answer is C. In his first year in Pittsburgh, he threw 4 touchdowns compared to 7 in his rookie year in Chicago. He was third team All ACC behind Lamar Jackson and Deshaun Watson.

27. The correct answer is A. Stroud was the 2nd player taken in the 2023 NFL draft after the Carolina Panthers selected Bryce Young. Fields was selected 11th overall by the Chicago Bears in the 2021 draft.

28. The correct answer is C. In his only year in Pittsburgh, Fields was 4-2 as a starter and experienced his career **best** completion percentage (65.8%), adjusted average yards per pass attempt (7.21) and passer rating (93.3).

29.     The correct answer is A. Nix played in 34 games for Auburn and 27 games for Oregon for a total of 61. Between the two schools he threw for 15,352 yards.

30.     The correct answer is A. Roethlisberger is the youngest quarterback to win a Super Bowl. He was 23 years 11 months and 3 days old when his Steelers won Super Bowl XL 21-10 over the Seattle Seahawks. Patrick Mahomes was 24 years 4 months and 14 days old when he won his first Super Bowl which was SB LIV.

31.     The correct answer is C. Bradford wore jersey #8 for the Rams, Vikings and Cardinals, however, he wore jersey #7 for the Philadelphia Eagles.

32.     The correct answer is C. While it's true, Bradford and McCoy have thrown for more yards and TDs in their NFL careers compared to Tebow, their career completion percentages are also higher. Bradford's is 62.5 and McCoy's is 62.6. Tebow's, in contrast, is only 47.9.

33.     The correct answer is B. Eli did not win NFL Comeback Player of the Year, however, Peyton did. He won it in 2012 after missing the 2011 season due to a neck injury.

34. The correct answer is C. Goff, did in fact, pass for more than 4,000 yards. He did it in 2 of his 5 seasons with the Rams, in 2018 and 2019.

35. The correct answer is B. While Hurts did finish second in the 2019 Heisman Trophy voting he lost out to quarterback Joe Burrow. DeVonta Smith won the award in 2020.

36. The correct answer is B. Sam Darnold is listed at a prototypical 6'3" and 225 lbs.

## Answers - Quarterbacks By Jersey Number

37. The NFL quarterback who wore jersey number 10 and has thrown for the most yards is Eli Manning. He has thrown for 57,023 yards for his career.

38. The NFL quarterback who wore jersey number 15 and has thrown for the most yards is Patrick Mahomes. In his 8 years with the Kansas City Chiefs Mahomes has thrown for 32,352 yards, 245 touchdowns and 74 interceptions through the 2024 season.

39. Patrick Mahomes wore jersey number 5 at Texas Tech. As a rookie with the Chiefs, the number 5 belonged to kicker Cairo Santos. The story is that Mahomes chose number 15 because it combined his favorite number 5 plus his draft position which was number 10. The Chiefs traded #1 picks with the Bills as well as giving them a third-round pick as well as the following year's first-round pick to move up to select Mahomes. Well worth it!

40.     Bart Starr of the Green Bay Packers was the winning quarterback of the first two Super Bowls in 1967 and 1968 (NFL-AFL Championships back then). As an indicator of the era in which he played, Starr's highest yardage total season was 1962 when he threw for 2,438 yards. He was enshrined into the Hall of Fame in 1977.

41.     The NFL quarterback who wore jersey number 7 and has thrown for the most yards is Ben Roethlisberger, with 64,088 yards. He played for the Pittsburgh Steelers from 2004-2021.

42.     The correct answer is D. Sonny Jurgensen threw for 255 touchdowns in career, slightly higher than Tony Romo's 248.

43.     The correct answer is C. Alex Smith does not have a Super Bowl ring. Drew Bledsoe has a ring from Super Bowl XXXVI winning it with the Patriots backing up Tom Brady. Mark Rypien earned not only a ring but a Super Bowl MVP as well from Super Bowl XXVI. Danny White has a ring as Roger Staubach's backup in Super Bowl XII.

44.     The correct answer is A. Aaron Rodgers, through the 2024 season, has a passer rating of 102.6. Tom Brady finished his career with a rating of 97.2

45.     Roger Staubach had a win percentage of 74.4%, threw for 22,279 yards and 152 touchdowns. He led the other 3 quarterbacks in each of those categories.

46.     John "Frenchy" Fuqua, who played from 1969 to 1976, was the intended target of Bradshaw's desperation pass. Fuqua was known as a stylish gentleman who would occasionally wear platform shoes with tropical fish swimming in his see-through heels.

47.     The correct answer is D. Stabler, not known as much of a running threat in the NFL, scampered 30 yards for the score to give the Raiders the lead setting up the dramatic finish.

48.     Earl Morrall who also previously backed up Johnny Unitas for Don Shula's Colts teams.

49.     Clint Longley went 11 for 20 for 203 yards and 2 touchdowns including a 50 yarder to Drew Pearson to win the game.

50.     Jim Kelly of the Buffalo Bills. His NFL high is 3,844 yards during the 1991 season. The other 3 quarterbacks have all passed for more than 4,000 yards in at least one season. Andrew Luck of the Colts did it 4 out of his 6 NFL seasons. Rich Gannon of the Raiders did it in 2002, and Joe Namath did it in 1967.

51. Zach Wilson, through the 2024 season, has thrown for 6,293 yards and 23 touchdowns through the 2024 season. Jamarcus Russell threw for 4,083 yards and 18 touchdowns while Manziel threw for only 1,675 yards and 7 touchdowns.

52. Tim Couch was selected number 1 overall by the Cleveland Browns in the 1999 draft. He played 5 NFL seasons compiling a 22-37 record throwing for 11,134 yards, 64 TDs and 67 interceptions.

53. Doug Flutie was picked in the 11th round of the 1985 draft by the Los Angeles Rams.

54. Doug Flutie played 14 seasons in the NFL, 1 less than Matt Ryan's 15.

55. The jersey numbers 1, 2, 6 and 19 have not been worn by a Super Bowl winning quarterback.

56. Kenny Picket wore jersey #8. His final game as a Steeler was in 2023. Tommy Maddox wore jersey #8 as well. His final game as a Steeler was in 2005.

57.     Donovan McNabb. He threw for a high of 3,916 yards in 2008 for the Philadelphia Eagles.

58.     Jeff Garcia went undrafted out of San Jose State. He made the Pro Bowl as a San Francisco 49er in 2000, 2001, and 2002. He also made the Pro Bowl as a Tampa Bay Buccaneer in 2007. He was Donavan McNabb's backup in the 2006 season and helped lead them to the playoffs while McNabb was injured.

59.     Anthony Richardson. Through the 2024 season, his second, Richardson's record as a starting quarterback is 8-7.

60.     Trey Lance. Through the 2024 season, he has only appeared in 12 games in his 3 years in the NFL.

61.     Dieter Brock. Brock had a stellar 10-year Canadian Football League career throwing for 34,830 yards prior to signing with the Rams. The year after, Brock injured his knee in the first preseason game, then aggravated his back shortly thereafter. He never played another down of football. He was 34 years old when he signed with the Rams.

62.     Cam Newton won the award in 2015 with the Carolina Panthers.

63. Phil Simms and Mark Rypien. Simms was MVP of Super Bowl XXI in 1987. Rypien was MVP of Super Bowl XXVI in 1992. Edelman, by the way, was MVP of Super Bowl LIII in 2019.

64. Mark Sanchez. Sanchez started in 6 playoff games as quarterback for the New York Jets leading them to the AFC Championship game in his two seasons there. He is 4 and 2 in the playoffs having lost in both AFC Championship games. Mayfield is currently 2-3 in his 5 playoff game starts, 2 with Cleveland and 3 with Tampa Bay. Cutler has only appeared in 2 playoff games and is 1-1.

65. Per profootballhof.com the correct answer is C. Jersey #16. The 11 names include quarterbacks George Blanda, Len Dawson, Joe Montana, and Kenny Stabler (he wore #16 with the Saints) as well as non-quarterbacks like Bronco Nagurski, Frank Gifford and 5 others (Ed Healey, George Musso, Duke Slater, Arnie Herber, and Walt Kiesling). Jersey #12 has 8 names so far including Bradshaw, Namath, Kelly, Staubach, Stabler and Griese plus 2 others (Arnie Herber, again, and William Roy Lyman).

## Answers - All Shapes, Sizes and Abilities

66. Kellen Moore of the Dallas Cowboys in 2015.

67. Steve Young was inducted in 2005

68. Steve Young and Boomer Esiason faced each other in Super Bowl XXIX in 1995 with Young and the Forty-Niners winning 49-26.

69. Todd Marinovich, out of USC, was selected by the Las Angeles Raiders with the 24th pick of the 1991 NFL draft.

70. David Humm – Nebraska, Bobby Douglass – Kansas, Tim Tebow – Florida, Mark Brunell – Washington.

71. Jim Zorn. Zorn was the Seattle Seahawks' very first quarterback in their inaugural season, often teaming with Hall of Famer Steve Largent.

72. Cade McNown was selected 12th overall in the 1999 draft by the Chicago Bears.

73. Ken Stabler won with the Oakland Raiders in 1977 in Super Bowl XI.

74. Tua Tagovailoa and Michael Penix Jr are the only left-handed starting quarterbacks.

75. Boomer Esiason. Esiason threw 247 touchdowns compared to Vick's 133, Stabler's 194, and Brunnell's 184.

76. Johnny Manziel. Manziel is listed at 6'0" tall while Flutie (5'10"), Young (5'10"), and Wilson (5'11") are all listed as being under six feet.

77. Jared Lorenzen. Lorenzen, known as "Hefty Lefty" signed as an undrafted free agent with the New York Giants in 2004 after throwing for 10,354 yards during his 4 years at the University of Kentucky. He was listed at 6'4" and 285lbs. He played for 2 seasons with the Giants earning a Super Bowl ring as Eli Manning's

backup in Super Bowl XLII. Lorenzen passed away at the age of 38 due to health issues.

78. Brock Osweiler and Paxton Lynch. Osweiler, who was measured at 6' 6-⅞", was selected 57th overall in the second round in 2012. Andrew Luck, Robert Griffin III, Ryan Tannehill, and Brandon Weeden were selected before him. Russell Wilson, at pick number 75, was selected after him by the Seattle Seahawks. Lynch, who was measured at 6' 6-⅝" was selected 26th overall in the first round in 2016. He was the third quarterback taken behind Jared Goff and Carson Wentz. Dak Prescott, at pick number 135, was selected by the Cowboys in the 4th round that same year.

79. Dan McGwire. McGwire, brother of former Oakland A's and St. Louis Cardinals Mark McGwire, was listed at 6' 8". The Seattle Seahawks selected him 16th overall in the 1991 draft out of San Diego State. He was the first quarterback taken in that draft. The only other quarterback selected in the first round was Todd Marinovich. Brett Favre would be selected at pick number 33 in the second round by the Atlanta Falcons. McGwire would go on to play 5 seasons in the NFL, all with the Seahawks, only starting 5 games.

80. Colin Kaepernick. Kaepernick is listed at 6'4" while Lawrence, Foles, and Flacco are all listed at 6'6".

81.     Justin Fields. Fields ran for 178 yards against the Miami Dolphins on November 6, 2022.


82.     Colin Kaepernick. Kaepernick rushed for 181 yards against the Green Bay Packers in the NFC Divisional playoff game on January 12, 2013.


83.     Lamar Jackson. Jackson, of the Baltimore Ravens, rushed for 1,206 during the 2019 season. He was NFL MVP that year. He also rushed for 1,005 yards the following year during the 2020 season.


84.     Lamar Jackson. Jackson rushed for 1,206 yards during the 2019 season.


85.     Bobby Douglass. Douglass, of the Chicago Bears, rushed 19 times for 100 yards and 4 touchdowns against the Green Bay Packers on November 4, 1973. The Bears won the game 31-17. Billy Kilmer, playing for the San Francisco Forty-Niners against the Minnesota Vikings performed the feat prior to the Super Bowl era on October 15, 1961 when he ran for 115 yards on 20 carries to go with his 4 touchdowns.

## Answers – Heismans, MVPs and Other Awards

86. Lamar Jackson and Cam Newton. Jackson won the Heisman Trophy in 2016 and was NFL MVP in 2019 and 2023. Newton won the Heisman Trophy in 2010 and was NFL MVP in 2015.

87. In 1970 Archie Manning finished 3rd behind winner Jim Plunkett of Stanford and runner up Joe Theisman of Notre Dame. In 2003 Eli Manning finished 3rd behind winner Jason White of Oklahoma and runner up Larry Fitzgerald of Pitt. Peyton Manning, of Tennessee, also lost out in the Heisman voting. In 1997 he finished second behind Charles Woodson of Michigan.

88. Peyton Manning. Manning has 5, the most in league history. He won the award in 2003, 2004, 2008, 2009, and 2013.

Brady has won it 3 times, Montana twice. Drew Brees did not win the award.

89.     Drew Brees. Brees finished second in the NFL MVP voting 4 times: 2006 (LaDanian Tomlinson was the winner), 2009 (Peyton Manning was the winner), 2011 (Aaron Rodgers was the winner) and 2018 (Patrick Mahomes was the winner). Tom Brady also finished second 4 times (2021, 2016, 2015, and 2013) but of course he won the award 3 times (2007, 2010, and 2017).

90.     Jim Kelly. Elway was NFL MVP in 1987, Esiason was NFL MVP the next year in 1988, and Marino was NFL MVP in 1984. Kelly was second in the NFL MVP voting in 1991 to his teammate Thurman Thomas.

91.     Joe Montana. Montana was voted to the Pro Bowl 7 times, Brees 13 times, Manning 14 times, and Brady, the career leader, 15 times.

92.     Bert Jones. Jones was selected by the Baltimore Colts 2nd overall (John Matuszak went #1 to the Houston Oilers) in the 1973 draft to replace an aging Johnny Unitas. He won the NFL MVP award after a stellar 1976 season, his fourth in the league.

93.     The correct answer is C. Troy Aikman never won the NFL MVP. Esiason was MVP in 1988, Ryan in 2016 and McNair in 2003.

94.     Craig Morton and Roger Staubach. Morton was selected out of Cal Berkeley fifth overall in the 1965 NFL draft. Staubach, on the other hand, was selected in the 10th round of the 1964 NFL draft as a "future" selection. The league allowed Staubach to be drafted because he was four years out of high school. He would fulfill his military commitment and play for the Cowboys beginning in 1969 as a 27-year-old rookie. Both would lead the Cowboys to Super Bowls as well as face each other in Super Bowl XII.

95.     Baker Mayfield. Even though he had scholarship offers coming out of high school at universities such as Washington State, Rice, New Mexico and Florida Atlantic, Mayfield chose to walk on at Texas Tech. He started as a true freshman for the Red Raiders. Mayfield transferred to Oklahoma in early 2014 walking on there as well. He became their starting quarterback in 2015 after sitting out a year.

96.     Charlie Ward and Jason White. Ward, who played at Florida State, won the Heisman Trophy in 1993. A two-sport star for the Seminoles, he was selected with the 26th pick in the first round of the 1994 NBA draft by the New York Knicks. He enjoyed a successful 11-year basketball career. White, who played at Oklahoma, won the Heisman Trophy in 2003. Concerns

regarding his injury history led to him not being drafted by an NFL team. He did eventually receive a tryout with the Kansas City Chiefs but was not signed.

97. Terry Bradshaw - inducted in 1989, John Elway - inducted in 2004, Troy Aikman - inducted in 2006, Peyton Manning - inducted in 2021.

98. Steve Spurrier, who won the award in 1966 after a great career at Florida where he would later coach. He left the Gators to sign a 5-year $25 million contract to become the head coach of the Washington Redskins in 2002.

99. Tom Brady of the New England Patriots unanimously won the award in 2010. This was his second after winning the award in 2007. The Patriots lost to the New York Jets in the playoffs that year. Lamar Jackson of the Baltimore Ravens won it in 2019. His team also lost in the playoffs that year. The Tennessee Titans defeated the Baltimore Ravens in the Divisional Round.

100. Brett Favre. Favre has thrown 336 interceptions in his career, more than any other quarterback in history. The next closest quarterback is George Blanda at 277, i.e., 59 fewer than Favre. In contrast, Joe Montana has thrown 139 and Troy Aikman has thrown 141 for a combined total of 280.

101. Jim Plunkett, the overall #1 draft pick of the New England Patriots, won two Super Bowls with the Raiders.

102. Three…as of this writing. All three played in the same general era and competed in the AFC. They are Dan Marino (Miami Dolphins), Jim Kelly (Buffalo Bills), and Dan Fouts (San Diego Chargers).

103. Warren Moon and Kurt Warner. Moon threw for 49,325 yards in his NFL career. Prior to his NFL career he threw for more than 21,228 yards in the Canadian Football League. He was not drafted by any NFL team after leading the Washington Huskies to victory over the Michigan Wolverines in the 1978 Rose Bowl. The bulk of his career was with the Houston Oilers. He also played for the Minnesota Vikings and Seattle Seahawks before ending his career with the Kansas City Chiefs. Warner threw for 32,344 yards playing for the Rams, Giants and Cardinals. He went undrafted after playing collegiately at Northern Iowa. He went on to become a two-time NFL MVP and Super Bowl MVP.

104. Lamar Jackson. Jackson, who won the award in 2016, was 19 years and 338 days old.

## Answers - Draft Selections

105. Chris Miller, selected with the 13th pick by the Atlanta Falcons in the 1987 draft; Akili Smith, selected with the 3rd pick by the Cincinnati Bengals in the 1999 draft; Joey Harrington, selected with the 3rd pick by the Detroit Lions in the 2002 draft; Marcus Mariota, selected with the 2nd pick by the Tennessee Titans in the 2015 draft; Justin Herbert, selected with the 6th pick by the Los Angeles Chargers in the 2020 draft; Bo Nix, selected with the 12th pick by the Denver Broncos in the 2024 draft.

106. Brady Quinn. The Cleveland Browns selected Quinn with the 22nd overall pick.

107. Ryan Tannehill was selected #8 overall by the Miami Dolphins and Brandon Weeden was selected with the 22nd pick by the Cleveland Browns.

108.  Joe Burrow, selected #1 overall by the Cincinnati Bengals, Tua Tagovailoa, selected #5 by the Miami Dolphins, Justin Herbert, the 6th pick taken by the Los Angeles Chargers, Jordan Love, picked by the Green Bay Packers with the 26th pick, and Jalen Hurts who was selected in the second round with pick #53 by the Philadelphia Eagles.

109.  The Redskins selected Kirk Cousins in the 4th round of that same draft.

110.  Jameis Winston and Marcus Mariota. Winston, the 2013 Heisman Trophy winner, was selected #1 overall by the Tampa Bay Buccaneers. Mariota, the 2014 Heisman Trophy winner, was taken with the second pick by the Tennessee Titans.

111.  Phillip Rivers had 421, Ben Roethlisberger had 418 while Eli Manning, the first player selected in their draft, had 366.

112.  Chad Kelly and Chandler Harnish. Kelly was selection number 253 in the last round of the 2017 draft. He was picked by the Denver Broncos. He spent 1 year at Clemson, 1 at East Mississippi and 2 years at Ole Miss. He spent a short time with both the Broncos and Colts before moving to the Canadien Football League. Harnish was also pick number 253 but selected by the Colts in the last round of the 2012 draft. He spent his college career at Northern Illinois University. He spent time with the Vikings and Cardinals before exiting the league in 2015.

113. J.P. Losman of Tulane was selected with the 22nd pick by the Buffalo Bills. Losman played for Buffalo for 5 years before spending 1 season each with Oakland, Seattle and Miami. In the 2006 season while at Buffalo, Losman started all 16 games for the Bills throwing for a respectable 3,051 yards 19 touchdowns and 14 interceptions. The Bills were 7-9 that year.

114. Heisman Trophy winner Andre Ware was selected with the 7th overall pick in the 1990 NFL draft by the Detroit Lions. In 4 years, he played in 6 games throwing for 1,112 yards. David Klingler was selected with the 6th overall pick two years later in the 1992 draft by the Cincinnati Bengals. He also played for the Oakland Raiders. In his 6 years in the league Klingler started 24 games throwing for 3,994 yards. Both played in the "Run and Shoot" offense at Houston under John Jenkins. Jenkins served as Jack Pardee's Offensive Coordinator before becoming head coach in 1990.

115. Kiper suggested, rather strongly, that the Colts should have taken Trent Dilfer out of Fresno State. The Tampa Bay Buccaneers selected him with the very next pick. Dilfer played for the Bucs for 6 seasons before signing with the Baltimore Ravens. In his only season with the team, he would lead them to victory in Super Bowl XXXV (although most would agree that team was actually led by Ray Lewis, Ed Reed and the rest of that defense). He then played for Seattle, Cleveland and San Francisco before retiring after 14 years in the league. Meanwhile, Alberts, who won the Butkus

Award as well as the Jack Lambert Trophy as a senior at Nebraska, played only a portion of 3 NFL seasons due to injury before retiring. Kiper's criticism of the Colts selection caused General Manager Bill Tobin to famously remark "Who in the hell is Mel Kiper anyway?"

116. Sam Bradford won it in 2010 followed by Cam Newton the following year. Kyler Murray was Offensive Rookie of the Year in 2019. It is interesting to note, Jayden Daniels, the 2024 Offensive Rookie of the Year, was selected with the second overall pick in the 2024 draft after the Chicago Bears selected Caleb Williams.

117. Archie Manning, out of Ole Miss, was selected by the Saints in the 1971 draft with the second overall pick. Jim Plunkett of Stanford was selected number one overall by the Boston Patriots with the Houston Oilers selecting Dan Pastorin out of Santa Clara with the third selection of that draft. While all three had great NFL careers, none of them are currently in the NFL Hall of Fame.

118. Dan McGwire of San Diego State, brother of the Oakland A's and St Louis Cardinal baseball star Mark McGwire, was selected by the Seattle Seahawks with the 16th pick while USC's Todd Marinovich was selected by the Los Angeles Raiders with the 24th pick. Favre was the 33rd pick. While 13 quarterbacks were selected in the draft, only Favre had a noteworthy career.

119. Tony Hunter, a tight end out of Notre Dame.

120. The Houston Gamblers. Kelly threw for a record 574 yards in a victory over Steve Young's L.A. Express on February 24, 1985. The USFL soon folded and Kelly joined the Bills, who retained his rights, in 1986.

121. Todd Blackledge. Blackledge was drafted with the 7th pick of the 1983 draft. He was the second QB taken after John Elway and ahead of Jim Kelly (14th) and Dan Marino (27th).

122. The correct answer is D. Aaron Rodgers. Rodgers was selected 24th overall by the Green Bay Packers in the 2005 draft. Dan Marino was selected 27th overall in the 1983 draft by the Miami Dolphins and Lamar Jackson was selected by the Baltimore Ravens with the 32nd overall pick in the 2018 draft. Drew Brees was also selected 32nd overall, albeit in the second round of the 2001 draft.

123. Chad Pennington, Giovanni Carmazzi, Chris Redman, Tee Martin, Marc Bulger, and Spergon Wynn.

124. The Colts did so 4 different times. John Elway in 1983, Jeff George in 1990, Peyton Manning in 1998, and Andrew Luck in 2012.

125. Ward, a West Columbia Texas native, spent his first year of college playing at the University of the Incarnate Word, a private Roman Catholic school in San Antonio. It was his only scholarship offer after averaging only 12 pass attempts his senior year in high school. After two years at Incarnate Word, Ward transferred to Washington State University reuniting with his Incarnate Word offensive coordinator.

126. Dillon Gabriel. Gabriel, who played in 64 games at UCF, Oklahoma and Oregon, threw for 18,722 yards 155 TDs and 32 interceptions. Shedeur Sanders threw for 14,327 yards, Dart 11,970 and Ward 11,281.

127. Both Oklahoma and Stanford can make the claim that they produced 3 quarterbacks that were the overall number one selection in their respective drafts. For Oklahoma they are Sam Bradford (2009 draft), Baker Mayfield (2018 draft), and Kyler Murray (2019 draft). For Stanford they are Jim Plunkett (1971 draft), John Elway (1983 draft), and Andrew Luck (2012 draft).

128. Carson Palmer. Heisman Trophy winning quarterback Palmer was selected number one overall by the Cincinnati Bengals in the 2003 draft. He would go on to be a 3-time Pro Bowler.

*Answers - Post Season Performances*

129. True. He has thrown 3 touchdowns and 8 interceptions.

130. The New York Giants beat Elway's Denver Broncos in Super Bowl XXI 39-20. The Washington Redskins beat the Broncos in Super Bowl XXII 42-10. The San Francisco Forty-Niners beat the Broncos in Super Bowl XXIV 55-10. Elway did become a Super Bowl Champion when the Broncos won back-to-back Super Bowls over the Packers and Falcons in SB XXXII and SB XXXIII.

131. Dan Fouts and Don Strock. Fouts, pilot of the Chargers "Air Coryell" offense, threw for 433 yards and 3 touchdowns. Don Strock, who came off the bench in relief of David Woodley, threw for 403 yards and 4 touchdowns. The Chargers would win the game 41-38 in overtime.

132. The Forty-Niners quarterback was Colin Kaepernick. Kaepernick was 16-28 for 302 yards, 1 touchdown and 1 interception. The Ravens quarterback was Joe Flacco. Flacco was 22-33 for 287 yards and 3 touchdowns with no interceptions. The Ravens, who entered the game as the underdog, won 34-31. Flacco was voted Super Bowl MVP.

133. Bob Griese. Despite playing in 3 consecutive Super Bowls and winning two, Griese was never voted the game's MVP.

134. The University of California at Berkeley, aka, Cal. Joe Kapp (Super Bowl IV with the Vikings), Craig Morton (Super Bowl V with the Cowboys and Super Bowl XII with the Broncos), Aaron Rodgers (Super Bowl XLV with the Packers), and Jared Goff (Super Bowl LIII) all played their collegiate careers at Cal. Vince Ferragamo, who quarterbacked the Los Angeles Rams to their first Super Bowl (SB XIV) played 2 years at Cal before transferring to Nebraska.

135. Daryle Lamonica (Super Bowl II), Joe Montana (Super Bowls XVI, XIX, XXIII, and XXIV), and Joe Theisman (Super Bowls XVII and XVIII) have all led teams to the Super Bowl. Montana won all 4 of his, Theisman was 1 and 1, and Lamonica was 0 and 1.

136. Len Dawson (Super Bowls I and IV), Bob Griese (Super Bowls VI, VII, and VIII), and Drew Brees (Super Bowl XLIV).

Dawson won one and lost one. Griese won 2 of his 3 and Brees won in his only Super Bowl appearance.

137. Ohio State. Washington State is represented by Mark Rypien and Drew Bledsoe. Rypien was MVP of Super Bowl XXVI with the Washington Redskins who defeated the Buffalo Bills. Bledsoe started for the New England Patriots against the Green Bay Packers in Super Bowl XXXI. Boston College is represented by Matt Hasselbeck and Matt Ryan. Hasselbeck's Seahawks lost to the Pittsburgh Steelers in Super Bowl XL. Ryan's Falcons lost a big lead and the game to the New England Patriots in Super Bowl LI. Maryland is represented by Boomer Esiason and Neil O'Donnell. Esiason's Bengals lost to the San Francisco Forty-Niners in Super Bowl XXIII. O'Donnell's Steelers lost to the Dallas Cowboys in Super Bowl XXX. Tom Tupa, who quarterbacked at Ohio State, did start Super Bowl XXXVII, however, it was as a punter, not at quarterback.

138. Craig Morton. Morton led both the Dallas Cowboys (Super Bowl V) and Denver Broncos (Super Bowl XII) to their first Super Bowls.

139. Jim Kelly. Unfortunately, his team lost all 4. Kelly quarterbacked the Buffalo Bills to Super Bowls, XXV, XXVI, XXVII, and XXVIII losing to the Giants, Redskins, Cowboys, then Cowboys again.

140. Vince Ferragamo. Ferragamo led the Rams against the Pittsburgh Steelers in Super Bowl XIV on January 20, 1980. The Steelers would go on to win 31-19 in a game much closer than the score indicates. The lead would change hands seven times. Pittsburgh would score two touchdowns in the fourth quarter to seal the victory. Ferragamo, who attended Cal Berkeley before transferring to Nebraska, would go 15 of 25 with no touchdowns and 1 interception.

141. Jake Delhomme and Cam Newton. Delhomme led the Panthers to Super Bowl XXXVIII against Tom Brady and the New England Patriots February 1, 2004. The Patriots won that game 32-29. Newton led them to Super Bowl 50 against Peyton Manning and the Denver Broncos on February 7, 2016. The Broncos won that game 24-10.

142. Stan Humphries. Humphries was a 6th round selection of the Washington Redskins in 1988 after a college career at Northeast Louisiana. He won a Super Bowl ring with the 'Skins as Mark Rypien's backup. He was traded to the Chargers prior to the 1992 season. He led the team that year to an 11-5 record. That team is the only one in NFL history to make the playoffs after starting 0-4. His 1994 team upset the Pittsburgh Steelers in the AFC Championship, sending the Chargers to Super Bowl XXIX against the San Francisco Forty-Niners on January 29, 1995. The Forty-Niners would go on to win that game 49-26. Humphries retired in 1997 after experiencing concussion issues.

143.   Craig Morton. Morton, of Cal Berkeley, was selected fifth overall in the 1965 NFL draft by the Dallas Cowboys. He primarily spent his first 4 years as the backup to Don Meredith. He led them to Super Bowl V on January 17, 1971 which the Baltimore Colts won 16-13 on Jim O'Brien's field goal with 5 seconds remaining.

144.   Peyton Manning won Super Bowl MVP honors after guiding the Indianapolis Colts to victory over the Chicago Bears in Super Bowl XLI in 2007. He also led the Denver Broncos to victory in Super Bowl 50 in 2016 over the Carolina Panthers.

145.   Peyton Manning. He won one (Super Bowl XLI vs the Chicago Bears in 2007) and lost one (Super Bowl XLIV vs the New Orleans Saints in 2010) with the Indianapolis Colts. He also won one (Super Bowl 50 vs the Carolina Panthers in 2016) and lost one (Super Bowl XLVIII vs the Seattle Seahawks in 2014) with the Denver Broncos.

146.   Peyton Manning. He played for Tony Dungy (Super Bowl XLI in 2007) and Jim Caldwell (Super Bowl XLIV in 2010) when he was with the Indianapolis Colts. He played for John Fox (Super Bowl XLVIII in 2014) and Gary Kubiak (Super Bowl 50 in 2016) when he was with the Denver Broncos.

147.   Steve Young. Young threw for 6 touchdowns in Super Bowl XXIX on January 29, 1995. He connected with Jerry Rice on 3 scores, Ricky Waters twice and William Floyd once. He was 24

of 36 for 325 yards and no interceptions. His passer rating was 134.8. He was also the Forty-Niners leading rusher that game with 49 yards on 5 carries. He was awarded the Super Bowl MVP.


148. Phillip Rivers. Rivers has thrown for 63,440 yards, good for sixth all time.


149. The score was 13-7 with the Pittsburgh Steelers winning on Franco Harris' historic catch and run. The game was played on December 23, 1972 in Pittsburgh.


150. Joe Theismann, Doug Williams, and Mark Rypien. Theismann quarterbacked them to victory in Super Bowl XVII in 1983. Doug Williams was at the helm in Super Bowl XXII in 1988. Mark Rypien led the team to victory in Super Bowl XXVI in 1992.


151. Tony Eason started Super Bowl XX against the Bears in 1986 but was soon replaced by Steve Grogan. The Patriots lost that game 46-10. Drew Bledsoe started Super Bowl XXXI in 1997 but lost to the Green Bay Packers 35-21.


152. Four different quarterbacks have led the Eagles in their five Super Bowl appearances. Ron Jaworski quarterbacked the Eagles in Super Bowl XV in 1981. The Oakland Raiders defeated the Eagles 27-10. Donovan McNabb quarterbacked the Eagles in Super Bowl XXXIX in 2005. The New England Patriots defeated

the Eagles 24-21. Nick Foles quarterbacked the Eagles in Super Bowl LII in 2018. The Eagles defeated the New England Patriots 41-33. Jalen Hurts quarterbacked the Eagles in Super Bowl LVII in 2023. The Kansas City Chiefs defeated the Eagles 38-35. He also quarterbacked the Eagles in Super Bowl LIX in 2025. The Eagles defeated the Kansas City Chiefs 40-22.

153. Jim Kelly had a playoff record of 9-8 and is the only one of that group with more playoff wins than losses. His losses are of course magnified by his losing 4 straight Super Bowls. Marino was 8-10, Fouts was 3-4, Moon was 3-7 and Rivers was 5-7.

154. Peyton Manning (Colts and Broncos), Tom Brady (Patriots and Buccaneers), Kurt Warner (Rams and Cardinals), and Craig Morton (Cowboys and Broncos). Manning and Brady both won with the two different teams. Warner won with the Rams but lost with the Cardinals. Morton lost the Super Bowl with both the Cowboys and the Broncos.

155. C.J. Stroud. Stroud, playing for the Ohio State Buckeyes, threw for 573 yards and 6 touchdowns in the 2022 Rose Bowl game against the Utah Utes.

156. Joe Burrow. Burrow threw for 463 yards and 5 touchdowns in the 2020 College Football Playoff National Championship game against the Clemson Tigers while playing for LSU. He also rushed for another score that game.

## Answers - Statistically Speaking

157.   Josh Allen. Mahomes has done it twice, throwing 50 TDs in 2018 and 41 in 2022. Burrow threw 43 TDs in 2024. Jackson threw 41 TDs in 2024. Allen's highest TD total is 37 which he did in 2020.

158.   Lamar Jackson. Jackson's career quarterback rating is 102.0 through 7 seasons. Joe Burrow's is 101.2 (5 seasons), Justin Herbert's is 96.7 (5 seasons), and Josh Allen's is 93.7 (7 seasons).

159.   Matthew Stafford and Matt Flynn combined to throw for 1,000 yards on January 1, 2012 when the Green Bay Packers hosted the Detroit Lions. The Packers won the game 45-41. Stafford threw for 480 yards and 5 touchdowns while Flynn, starting in what would be his last game as a Packer, threw for 520 yards and 6 touchdowns.

160. Eli Manning and Drew Brees combined to throw for 13 touchdowns on November 1, 2015 with the Saints winning 52-49 in New Orleans. Manning threw 6 touchdowns to go with his 350 yards while Brees threw for 7 touchdowns and 505 yards.

161. Drew Bledsoe with 70. In a November 13, 1994 game between Bledsoe's Patriots and Warren Moon's Minnesota Vikings, Bledsoe was 45-70 for 426 yards and 3 touchdowns. The Patriots beat the Vikings 26-20. They had only 12 rushing attempts for the game. Warren Moon, by the way, was 26-42 for 349 and 1 touchdown.

162. (1) Drew Brees - 97.1 (18 games), (2) Joe Montana - 95.6 (23 games), (3) Tom Brady - 89.8 (48 games), (4) Peyton Manning - 87.4 (27 games).

163. Tom Brady. Brady had 46, 3 more than Peyton Manning. Ben Roethlisberger had the most with one team (Pittsburgh Steelers). He had 41.

164. Tom Brady. Brady had 58, 4 more than Peyton Manning. Ben Roethlisberger had the most with one team (Pittsburgh Steelers). He had 53. Drew Brees, who played for the Chargers and Saints, also had 53.

165. Bert Jones, Warren Moon and Donovan McNabb were all sacked 12 times in one game. Jones, while playing for the Baltimore Colts against the St. Louis Cardinals on October 26, 1980. Moon, while playing for the Houston Oilers against the Dallas Cowboys on September 29, 1985. McNabb, while playing for the Philadelphia Eagles against the New York Giants on September 30, 2007.

166. Vinny Testaverde threw 35 interceptions in 1988 while playing for the Tampa Bay Buccaneers.

167. Vinny Testaverde has led the NFL in passes intercepted in 4 separate seasons on 3 different teams. In 1988 he threw 35 picks. In 1989 he threw 22 (tied with Dan Marino). Those two years he was early in his career with the Tampa Bay Buccaneers. In 2000 he threw 25 while quarterbacking the New York Jets and in 2004 he threw 20 with the Dallas Cowboys.

168. Aaron Rodgers. In 2018, Rodgers threw 402 passes without an interception until the Chicago Bears' free safety Eddie Jackson intercepted him in a week 15 game at Soldier Field in Chicago. The Bears would go on to win the game 24-17. The Packers would finish the season that year with a 6-9-1 record.

169. Matt Ryan. Ryan threw for 62,792 yards, primarily with the Atlanta Falcons. His career spanned from 2008 to 2022. Dan Marino threw for 61,361. He played for the Miami Dolphins from

1983 to 1999. John Elway threw for 51,475 yards. He played for the Denver Broncos from 1983 to 1998. Going into the 2025 season, Russell Wilson is at 46,135 yards.


170.    Warren Moon. His record as a starting quarterback is 102 wins and 101 losses. Joe Namath was 66-70 with 4 ties and Boomer Esiason was 80-93. Eli Manning was 117-117 during the regular season but his 8-4 playoff record helped him earn 2 Super Bowl victories.


171.    Tom Brady and Ben Roethlisberger. Brady, then with the New England Patriots, threw for 505 yards in Super Bowl LII against the Philadelphia Eagles on February 4, 2018. Roethlisberger of the Pittsburgh Steelers threw for 501 yards in the AFC Wild Card game against the Cleveland Browns on January 10, 2021. Both the Patriots and the Steelers lost those games. SIDENOTE: Roethlisberger threw 4 interceptions that same game. Brady lost that Super Bowl featuring the "Philly Special" or "Philly Philly", a flea flicker caught by Nick Foles.


172.    Tom Brady. Brady threw for 5,235 yards in 2011 while with the New England Patriots and 5,316 yards in 2021 while with the Tampa Bay Buccaneers.


173.    Kerry Collins - 40,992 yards, Jay Cutler - 35,133 yards, Ryan Tannehill - 34,881 yards, Phil Simms - 33,462 yards

174. Tom Brady. Brady has thrown for 649 career touchdowns in his illustrious career. Jim Kelly (237 TDs), Steve Young (232 TDs) and Joe Namath (173 TDs) combined to throw a total 642 touchdowns. This is one of those stats that doesn't sound real but is!

175. Brett Favre - Favre played 20 years in the NFL for the Packers, Vikings and Jets.

176. Matthew Stafford. Stafford has 38 4th quarter comebacks which ties him with Matt Ryan for 4th all time.

177. Russell Wilson. Wilson has 40 through the 2024 season while Rodgers has 34, Cousins 31, and Flacco 28.

178. Jimmy Garoppolo. Garoppolo's career passing yards per attempt mark is 8.2. This is followed by Steve Young at 8.0 and Kurt Warner and Tony Romo at 7.9.

179. Drew Brees. Brees exceeded the 5,000-yard mark in the 2008, 2011, 2012, 2013, and 2016 seasons.

180. Drew Brees. Brees exceeded the 4,000-yard mark in every season from 2006 through 2017. During that stretch he threw for

58,097 yards and averaged, yes averaged an astounding 4,841 yards per season.

181. Kyler Murray. Murray recovered 13 fumbles during the 2021 season.

182. Drew Brees. His highest total was 46 in 2011. Patrick Mahomes threw for 50 TDs in 2018. Tom Brady threw for 50 TDs in 2007. Peyton Manning holds the single season TD pass record throwing for 55 touchdowns in 2013.

183. Aaron Rodgers. Rodgers has been sacked 571 times going into the 2025 season. This is 1 more than Fran Tarkenton and 6 more than Tom Brady. Russell Wilson is 4th with 560.

## Answers - "Name" That Quarterback

184. C.J. Beathard. Beathard, who's initials C.J. stand for Casey Jarrett, was named after his father Casey Beathard who has written or co-written country music for the likes of Kenny Chesny (such as "No shoes, no shirt, no problem"), Trace Adkins and Tracy Lawrence. Casey Beathard himself is the son of Bobby Beathard, Hall of Fame football executive most notably as general manager of the Washington Redskins and San Diego Chargers. Bobby Beathard's younger brother, Pete, was an NFL quarterback with several NFL teams in the 60's and 70's.

185. Rayne Dakota Prescott. Prescott has gone by "Dak" or "Dakota" since childhood to avoid the teasing at the hands of other children.

186. Coleridge Bernard Stroud IV. CJ has gone by "CJ" since birth.

187. These are the teams the quarterbacks ended their careers with: Matt Leinhart – Oakland Raiders, Matt Schaub – Atlanta Falcons, Matt Hasselback – Indianapolis Colts, Matt Cassel – Detroit Lions, and Matt Ryan – Indianapolis Colts.

188. Matt Ryan threw for 4,000 yards or more for 10 consecutive seasons from 2011 to 2020.

189. Steve DeBerg. DeBerg threw for 34,231 yards during a career that spanned from 1978 to 1998 with 6 different teams. Steve Young is second with 33,124. Young has more career passing yards if including the playoffs.

190. Joe Flacco has thrown for more yards than the other "average Joes" by far! Flacco has thrown for 45,697 yards (and counting), Kapp, 5,911 yards, Ferguson, 29,817 yards, and Theisman, 25,206 yards.

191. Billy Joe Tolliver. Tolliver threw for 10,760 yards in his career while Hobert threw for 3,371.

192. Drew Stanton had the highest average yards per pass completion at 11.8. Bledsoe is next at 11.6, followed by Brees, 11.3, and Lock, 11.0.

193. Chris Weinke. In his rookie year with the Carolina Panthers, Weinke threw for 2,931 yards, 11 touchdowns and 19 INTs.

194. Jeff George. Hostetler was a Pro Bowler in 1994, Blake in 1995, and Garcia in 2000, 2001, 2002, and 2007.

195. Joe Namath (Super Bowl III), Joe Theisman (Super Bowl XVII), Joe Montana (Super Bowls XVI, XIX, XXIII, and XXIV), and Joe Flacco (Super Bowl XLVII).

196. Tommy Kramer. DeVito played for the giants in 2023 and 2024 and is currently on their 2025 roster. He has thrown for 1,101 yards, 8 touchdowns and 3 interceptions. Tommy Maddox played for the Giants in 1995 going 6 off 23 for 49 yards, no touchdowns and 3 interceptions.

197. Bobby Hebert. Hebert made the Pro Bowl in 1993 his first year with the Atlanta Falcons after spending the first 7 years of his career with the New Orleans Saints.

198. Billy Kilmer. Kilmer's best passing season was 1969 when he was with the New Orleans Saints. That year he threw for 2,532 yards, 20 touchdowns and 17 interceptions.

199. Steve Bartkowski. Spurrier, who backed up John Brodie, played there from 1967-1975, Steve DeBerg, who preceded Joe Montana, was a Niner from 1978-1980, and Steve Bono, who backed up Joe Montana, was there from 1989-1993. Bartkowski, on the other hand, spent the first 11 years of his career with the Falcons before playing one final season with the Rams.

200. Joe Kapp of the Minnesota Vikings who lost to the Kansas City Chiefs in Super Bowl IV, Joe Theisman of the Washington Redskins who lost to the Los Angeles Raiders in Super Bowl XVIII, and Joe Burrow of the Cincinnati Bengals who lost to the Los Angeles Rams in Super Bowl LVI.

201. Vince Ferragamo. Ferragamo started 53 games in his career, mostly with the Rams. He threw for 11,336 yards, 76 touchdowns and 91 interceptions. Young threw for 8,964 yards, 46 touchdowns and 51 interceptions while Evans threw for 9,485 yards, 52 touchdowns and 74 interceptions. All three quarterbacks threw for more interceptions than touchdowns in their careers.

## Answers - One For Each Team

202. Cam Newton. In the 2015 NFC Divisional round, Newton led the Panthers over the Seattle Seahawks 31-24. They would later play in Super Bowl 50 against the Denver Broncos losing 24-10.

203. Joey Harrington, who would make most of the starts that season, his only one with the team, Byron Leftwich who also spent only one year in Atlanta, and Chris Redman, who played with the Falcons for 4 years.

204. Daniel Jones. Jones' completion percentage with the Giants was 64.1. Kurt Warner's was 62.8 during his one season (2004) with the team. Eli Manning's was 60.3 and Phil Simms' was 55.4.

205. The Saints were 3-13 that year, a year in which they did not play in New Orleans because of the damage caused by Hurricane Katrina.

206. Steve McNair. McNair was selected with the 3rd overall pick in the 1995 draft by the Houston Oilers. In 1997 the Oilers moved to Nashville and adopted the name Tennessee Oilers for that season as well as the 1998 season. The team then changed their name to the Tennessee Titans beginning with the 1999 season. McNair played for Tennessee through the 2005 season.

207. T.J. Yates. During the 2011 season, starter Matt Schaub and backup Matt Leinhart became injured. Yates became the starter the rest of the season and into the playoffs. He guided them to a Wild Card victory over the Cincinnati Bengals before losing the following week to the Baltimore Ravens in the Divisional Round.

208. Mark Brunell. Brunell, who quarterbacked the team from 1995-2003, led the Jaguars to 4 playoff wins; 2 in 1996, 1 in 1998, and 1 in 1999.

209. Jay Fiedler. Fiedler's record was 36-23. Fitzpatrick was 9-11, Pennington was 12-8, and Chad Henne was 13-18.

210. Kerry Collins. In what would be his final season, Collins started the season opener, a 34-7 loss to the Houston Texans. He would play in only two more games that season, giving way to Curtis Painter and Dan Orlovsky.

211. Brandon Moore who was the right guard on the play blocking the New England Patriots Vince Wilfork.

212. Joe Theisman. In Super Bowl XVII, Theisman was 15 of 23 for 143 yards and 2 touchdowns with 2 interceptions. In Super Bowl XXII, Doug Williams was 18 of 29 for 340 yards 4 touchdowns, and 1 interception. In Super Bowl XXVI Mark Rypien was 18 of 33 for 292 yards, 2 touchdowns and 1 interception. Both Williams and Rypien earned game MVP honors.

213. Carson Wentz. In his rookie campaign, Wentz started 16 games and was 379-607 for 3,782 yards, 16 touchdowns and 14 interceptions. Kolb threw zero touchdowns, Cunningham threw 1, and McNabb threw 8 in their respective rookie years.

214. Tyrod Taylor. Taylor, who played for the Bills from 2015-2017, was a replacement selection in 2015. Tom Brady and Ben Roethlisberger were voted in but did not play. That year, Taylor threw for 3,035 yards, 20 touchdowns and 6 interceptions.

215. Mac Jones. Jones made the Pro Bowl in 2021. He was selected by the Pats with the 15th pick in the 2021 draft.

216. Neil O'Donnell. O'Donnell, a 1992 Pro Bowler, was 28-49 for 239 yards and 1 touchdown. He did however throw 3

interceptions, 2 to Larry Brown in the second half which the Cowboys then converted into touchdowns.

217. Kyle Boller. Boller, who was drafted by the Ravens and played for them from 2003 through the 2007 season, started 42 games. Harbaugh started 12 games in 1998, Dilfer started only 8 games, all during the Raven's 2000 Super Bowl season, and Banks started 18 during parts of the 1999 and 2000 seasons.

218. Jake Plummer. Plummer started 54 games ('03-'06) while Brian Griese started 51 ('00-'02), Cutler started 37 ('06-'08), and Kyle Orton started 33 ('09-'11).

219. Steve Fuller. Fuller, out of Clemson and selected 23rd overall in the first round by the Chiefs in the 1979 NFL draft, threw 6 touchdowns and 14 interceptions during his rookie campaign. Those records still stand. Patrick Mahomes played in only one game his rookie year as a back-up to Alex Smith.

220. Terrelle Pryor. Pryor was selected in the 3rd round of the 2011 supplemental draft after a tumultuous career at Ohio State.

221. Christian Ponder. Ponder threw for 6,658 yards during his 4 seasons with the team (2011-2014). Gannon threw for 6,457 yards (1987-1992), Bridgewater 6,150 yards (2014-2017), and Cunningham 5,680 (1997-1999).

222. Jay Cutler. Cutler threw for 23,443 yards. In comparison, McMahon threw for 11,203 and Harbaugh threw for 11,567 for a total of 22,770.

223. Kurt Warner. Warner was honored with both at the end of the 2008 season.

224. Jeff George. All the others played and started for the Detroit Lions.

225. Don Horn, Lynn Dickey, and Matt Flynn. Horn threw for 410 yards on December 21, 1969 against the St. Louis Cardinals. Lynn Dickey threw for 418 yards on October 12, 1980 against the Tampa Bay Buccaneers. Matt Flynn threw for 520 yards on January 1, 2012 against the Detroit Lions.

226. Joe Burrow of LSU in 2020 and Carson Palmer of USC in 2003.

227. Jack Thompson, the "Throwin' Samoan", in 1984, and Akili Smith in 1999.

228. Trent Dilfer. Dilfer, the Buccaneer's #6 overall selection in the 1994 draft, would play for the Bucs for 6 seasons going to the Pro Bowl in 1997.

229. Scott Mitchell, Jon Kitna, Matthew Stafford and Jared Goff. Mitchel threw for 4,338 yards in 1995. Kitna did it in back-to-back years, throwing for 4,208 in 2006 and 4,068 in 2007. Matthew Stafford did it 7 consecutive seasons from 2011-2017 and also did it in 2020. His highest season total was in 2011 when he threw for 5,038 yards. Jared Goff, so far, has done it 3 consecutive years from 2022-2024. His highest season total to date was in 2024 when he threw for 4,629 yards.

230. Joe Montana. Elvis Grbac threw for 4,169 yards in 2000. Trent Green hit the mark three consecutive years from 2003-2005 throwing for 4,039, 4,531, and 4,014 yards during those years. Alex Smith threw for 4,042 in 2017. Montana's highest yardage total as a Chief was 3,283 in 1994. He also never surpassed the 4,000-yard mark in any season with the San Francisco Forty-Niners.

231. Jeff Garcia. Garcia, who quarterbacked the Forty-Niners from 1999-2003, threw for 16,408 yards and 113 touchdowns while with the team. Smith, on the Niner roster from 2005-2012, threw for 14,280 yards and 81 scores. Garoppolo, with the team from 2017-2022, threw for 13,599 yards and 82 TDs.

232. In order they are: Tony Romo – 34,183 yards, Troy Aikman – 32,942, Roger Staubach – 22,700, and Danny White – 21,959.

233. Baker Mayfield. Mayfield was 29-30 with the Browns from 2018-2021. Bernie Kosar was 53-51 from 1985-1993. Vinny Testaverde was 16-15 from 1993-1995 and Brian Sipe was 57-55 from 1974-1983.

234. Freddie Solomon. Solomon slipped on his break so Montana went to his secondary receiver Clark. To hit Clark, he had to throw it over Ed "Too Tall" Jones.

235. Jim Everett. Everett played for the Rams from 1986-1993 and threw for 23,758. If you were expecting it to be Kurt Warner, you'll be disappointed to know that he is 7th on the list.

236. Tavaris Jackson. Jackson, who was an unrestricted free agent after his stint with the Minnesota Vikings, signed a 2-year deal in 2011 with the 'Hawks and was immediately announced as the starter. That season he would throw for 3,091 yards, 14 touchdowns and 13 interceptions. Russell Wilson was drafted the following year and became the starter.

## *Answers - Bonus Baby!*

237. Rich Gannon and Joe Flacco. Gannon played 17 years for the Vikings, Chiefs and Raiders. He was the 2002 NFL MVP after throwing for 4,689 yards leading the Oakland Raiders to the Super Bowl. Flacco has played for 17 years going into the 2025 season. He was MVP of Super Bowl XLVII guiding the Baltimore Ravens to victory over the San Francisco Forty-Niners on February 3, 2013.

238. Don Majkowski. Known as the "Majik Man", Majkowski was the starter in 1992 when on September 20th against the Cincinnati Bengals he injured his ankle in the first quarter. Favre came in and was the starter for the next 16 years.

239. Drew Brees (Super Bowl XLIV in 2010) and Nick Foles (Super Bowl LII in 2018) both attended Austin Texas' Westlake High School.

240. Tom Brady and Barry Bonds both went to Junipero Serra High School in San Mateo, California.


241. Fitzpatrick played for 9 teams from 2005 through the 2021 season. Those teams are St. Louis Rams, Cincinnati Bengals, Buffalo Bills, Tennessee Titans, Houston Texans, New York Jets, Tampa Bay Buccaneers, Miami Dolphins and the Washington Football Team (now known as the Washington Commanders).


242. Harvard University. At Harvard, Fitzpatrick was the 2004 Ivy League Player of the Year. He was drafted in the 7th round of the 2005 draft, the last quarterback taken. That was the same draft that included Alex Smith and Aaron Rodgers.


243. The "K-Gun". Many thought it was named after Kelly, however, it was actually named after the tight end, Keith McKeller who in their no-huddle formations, could be found to line up in a variety of different positions to create mismatches.


244. Josh Allen accomplished this feat December 1, 2024 against the San Francisco Forty-Niners. Allen's Bills won the game 35-10. The passing touchdown came on a play where Allen passed to Amari Cooper who, when tackled, lateralled the ball back to Allen who ran it in for the score.

245. Josh Allen of the Buffalo Bills against the San Francisco Forty-Niners on December 1, 2024 (Buffalo won 35-10). Bo Nix of the Denver Broncos against the Baltimore Ravens on November 3, 2024 (Baltimore won 41-10). Jared Goff of the Detroit Lions against the Seattle Seahawks on September 30, 2024 (Detroit won 42-29).

246. Chris Chandler and Ryan Fitzpatrick. Chandler has thrown touchdown passes for 8 teams (7 franchises): The Indianapolis Colts, Tampa Bay Buccaneers, Phoenix Cardinals, Los Angeles Rams, Houston Oilers, Atlanta Falcons, Chicago Bears and the St. Louis Rams. Fitzpatrick has thrown touchdown passes for 8 teams (8 franchises): The St. Louis Rams, Cincinnati Bengals, Buffalo Bills, Tennessee Titans, Houston Texans, New York Jets, Tampa Bay Buccaneers, and the Miami Dolphins.

247. The Washington Football Team. Fitzpatrick joined them signing a one-year deal for the 2021 season. In the season opener against the Chargers, he went 3-6 for 13 yards, no touchdowns and no interceptions before he hurt his hip in the second quarter. He did not return to the game and was put on injured reserve for the season. He would retire the following summer.

248. Sean Payton, coach of the Denver Broncos, went 8 for 23 for 79 yards in 3 games that season. He did throw 1 interception against, you guessed it, the New Orleans Saints who he would later coach to a Super Bowl victory.

249. Jim Harbaugh, Kellen Moore, Kliff Kingsbury, and Kevin O'Connell all saw the field as an NFL quarterback. Harbaugh, a Michigan star, played 14 years in the NFL with the Bears, Colts, Ravens and Chargers throwing for 26,288 yards and 129 touchdowns. Moore signed as an undrafted free agent with the Detroit Lions in 2012 out of Boise State. He later joined the Dallas Cowboys where he played 3 games in 2015 throwing for 779 yards with 4 touchdowns. Kingsbury was selected in the 6th round of the 2003 draft by the New England Patriots after throwing for 12,429 yards at Texas Tech including 5,017 yards as a senior. He would not play in a game until he landed with the New York Jets in 2005 playing in the 4th quarter of a late November game against the Broncos. Kingsbury would go 1 for 2 for 17 yards in his only NFL appearance. O'Connell was selected in the 3rd round of the 2008 draft by the New England Patriots after a solid collegiate career at San Diego State. He appeared in 2 games as a rookie going 4 of 6 for 23 yards.

250. His very first pass was as a Green Bay Packer in the second game of the 1992 season. Favre threw a pass that was deflected which he then caught for a 7-yard loss.

251. Norman Julius Esiason.

252. Rodney Peete of USC. Peete's Trojans beat Aikman's UCLA Bruins in both his junior and senior seasons. Peete was second to Barry Sanders in the Heisman voting while Aikman was third. He

was selected by the Detroit Lions in the 6th round of the 1989 draft. He would play for 6 teams in his 15-year NFL career.


253. Marc Wilson. Wilson, who primarily played for the Raiders, averaged 13.3 yards per completed pass in his NFL career. Steve Young averaged 12.4 yards while Jim McMahon averaged 12.2 yards.


254. Fran Tarkenton. In an October 27, 1974 game against the Patriots, the Minnesota Vikings' Tarkenton scored on a 3-yard bootleg. After running into the end zone to give the Vikings a 14-10 lead, he turned and spiked the ball off the helmet of Patriot cornerback Ron Bolton. Both players were ejected after a fight ensued. The Patriots went on to win the game 17-14.


255. Trent Dilfer. In a 1995 game between the Tampa Bay Buccaneers and the Minnesota Vikings, Dilfer was ejected after receiving a personal foul penalty for delivering a blow to the head of the Vikings John Randle. With the Vikings leading the Bucs 28-7 in the third quarter, Randle chased Dilfer out of the pocket causing him to throw the ball away. In the process, Randle tackled Dilfer around the knees, knocking the quarterback to the ground. Dilfer originally thought it was a cheap shot (he later admits it wasn't but that frustration got the best of him) and so jumped on Randle while Randle lay on the ground.

256. John Wolford. Wolford signed with the New York Jets as an undrafted free agent in 2018 after his playing career at Wake Forest. He was waived by the Jets and then spent time with the Arizona Hotshots of the Alliance of American Football league. In 2020 he signed with the Rams and held a roster spot through the 2022 season. He passed for 626 yards his 3 years with the Rams going 61-104 with 1 touchdown and 5 interceptions.

257. True. Brady had 35 career playoff wins. Peyton Manning had 14, Eli Manning had 8, and Troy Aikman had 11 for a total of 33.

258. Tommy Kramer and Erik Kramer. Tommy played 14 seasons including 13 with the Minnesota Vikings and 1 with the New Orleans Saints. Erik Kramer played 10 seasons including 1 with the Atlanta Falcons, 3 with the Detroit Lions, 5 with the Chicago Bears and 1 with the San Diego Chargers.

259. Mark Clayton and Mark Duper, AKA "The Marks Brothers". That year Clayton caught 73 balls for 1,389 yards while Duper caught 71 balls for 1,206 yards. Both receivers were small in stature for the position standing 5'9" with Duper listed at 185 pounds and Clayton at 177 pounds.

260. Fran Tarkenton. Tarkenton did two tours of duty with the Vikings totaling 13 seasons. During those seasons he threw for

33,098 yards. Second on that list is Tommy Kramer at 24,775 yards.

261. Randy Moss, who played for the Vikings from 1998 to 2010.

262. Drew Brees (5,476), Tom Brady (5,235), and Matthew Stafford (5,038) all surpassed the 5,000-yard benchmark during the 2011 season.

## Answers – But Wait, There's More…A Lot More!

263. Lamar Jackson. Jackson, through the 2024 season, has rushed for 6,173 yards.

264. Lamar Jackson, Michael Vick, Cam Newton and Russell Wilson have each surpassed Chicago Bears great Gayle Sayers who had only 4,956 yards rushing. Through the 2024 season, Jackson had 6,173 yards, Vick had 6,109, Newton had 5,628 and Wilson has 5,462.

265. The correct answer is C. The 2017 National Treasures NFL Shield Patrick Mahomes Autographed Rookie Card #161 was sold in July 2021 for $4.3 million by PWCC Marketplace.

266. The correct answer is Andrew Luck. Elway was NFL MVP in 1987 as well as being named to the Pro Bowl 9 times. Brodie was NFL MVP in 1970 the same year he was named All-Pro. Plunkett was Super Bowl XV MVP. Luck, while never an MVP,

was a 4-time Pro Bowler as well as 2018's Comeback Player of the Year.

267. Steve Dils. Dils played 10 years in the NFL playing for the Vikings, Rams, and Falcons. Schonert played 9 years for the Bengals and Falcons. Stenstrom played 4 years for the Vikings. Davis Mills is about to start his 5th season with the Texans.

268. Stewart played 8 years for the Steelers before playing 1 season for the Bears and 2 seasons for the Ravens before retiring in 2005.

269. The three quarterbacks who played for the University of Florida and who won the Heisman Trophy are Steve Spurrier (1966), Danny Wuerffel (1996), and Tim Tebow (2007).

270. After his one season with the Jets, Tebow was signed by the New England Patriots only to be released on the last day of cuts in 2013. He would then sign with the Eagles in the spring of 2015 but was released after the last preseason game. After being out of football for 6 years the Jaguars signed him as an experiment. They wanted to make a tight end out of him. He was released prior to the start of the regular season.

271. The 4 Heisman Trophy quarterbacks who played for Oklahoma are Jason White (2003), Sam Bradford (2008), Baker Mayfield (2017) and Kyler Murray (2018).

272. Troy Smith is the only Buckeye to win the Heisman. He was drafted in the 5th round of the 2007 NFL draft by the Baltimore Ravens (Sidenote: JaMarcus Russell was the overall number one selection that year). He played there for 3 seasons before playing

one year for the San Francisco Forty-Niners where he ended his career.

273. Dwayne Haskins. Haskins threw for 4,831 yards, 50 touchdowns and 8 interceptions that year for the Buckeyes. He was then selected by the Washington Redskins (now Commanders) with the 15th overall pick in the 2019 draft.

274. Vinny Testaverde and Gino Torretta. Testaverde won the Heisman in 1986. He was then selected by the Tampa Bay Buccaneers with the first overall pick in the 1987 draft. Torretta won the Heisman in 1992. He was selected in the 7th round of the 1993 draft by the Minnesota Vikings.

275. Of the 55 touchdown passes only 3 went to a running back. All 3 were to Knowshon Moreno. Manning threw 14 to WR Demaryius Thomas, 12 to TE Julius Thomas, 11 to WR Eric Decker, and 10 to Slot Receiver Wes Welker. He threw 3 to WR Andre Caldwell, 1 to TE Jacob Tamme and 1 to TE Joel Dreessen.

276. The correct answer is all 4 of them have beaten all 32 NFL teams. This is possible of course since they all played for more than one team. Brady played for the Patriots and Buccaneers, Manning for the Colts and Broncos, Favre for the Packers, Jets and Vikings and Brees played for the Chargers and Saints.

277. In Rodger's illustrious 20-year career, he has thrown only 116 regular season interceptions (again, through the 2024 season) and has had only 4 seasons where he has thrown 10 or more. In

comparison Drew Brees also played for 20 years. Brees threw 10 or more interceptions in 14 of them.

278. Peyton Manning. Manning threw 28 INTs in his 1998 rookie year and 23 during the 2001 season. Brees threw 22 in 2010 (and still made the Pro Bowl). Neither Rodgers or Brady has thrown more than 20 interceptions in a season (at least through the 2024 season).

279. The first to wear that number and win league MVP was Brian Sipe of the Cleveland Browns. Sipe played for the Browns from 1974 to 1983 throwing for 23,713 yards, 154 touchdowns and 149 interceptions. He won the award in 1980 when he threw for 4,132 yards, 30 touchdowns and 14 interceptions.

280. The player who last wore jersey number 12 for the Patriots before Tom Brady was another Tom. Tom Ramsey wore number 12 from 1986 through 1988. Ramsey was a quarterback who started his career with the L.A. Express of the USFL after quarterbacking the UCLA Bruins.

281. The player who last wore jersey number 12 for the Green Bay Packers before Aaron Rodgers is Lynn Dickey. Dickey played for the Packers retiring in 1985. His best season was 1983 when he threw for 4,458 yards, 32 touchdowns and 29 interceptions. His average yards per completion that year was 15.4!

282. True. Even though Young and Vick are known for their running ability and Moon and Marino are known as pure passers, all four have an average yards per pass completion rate of 12.4.

283. Ken Anderson, who many believe should be in the Hall of Fame, wore jersey number 14 for the Bengals after being drafted in the 3rd round out of Augustana, a private Lutheran college in Rock Island, Illinois.

284. Matthew Stafford, Ben Roethlisberger, and Jameis Winston. Stafford threw for 5,038 yards in 2011 while with the Detroit Lions. That year the NFC Pro Bowl quarterbacks were Aaron Rodgers, Drew Brees, Cam Newton and Eli Manning. Roethlisberger threw for 5,129 yards in 2018 leading the entire league in that category. The AFC Pro Bowl quarterbacks that year were Patrick Mahomes, Andrew Luck, Deshaun Watson, and Tom Brady. Jameis Winston threw for 5,109 yards in 2019 while with the Tampa Bay Buccaneers. The NFC Pro Bowl quarterbacks that year were Aaron Rodgers, Russell Wilson, Drew Brees, and Kirk Cousins.

285. The five quarterbacks taken, in order, were Tim Couch (#1 to the Browns), Donovan McNabb (#2 to the Eagles), Akili Smith (#3 to the Bengals), Daunte Culpepper (#11 to the Vikings), and Cade McNown (#12 to the Bears).

286. Steve DeBerg. DeBerg, who played in 206 games from 1978 to 1998 (with a gap from 1994 to 1997) was 53-86-1 as a starter of 140 games.

287. Both Warren Moon and Matt Schaub. Moon, in 1990 playing for the Houston Oilers, threw for 527 yards against the Kansas City Chiefs in a 27-10 win at Arrowhead. Shaub, in 2012 playing for the Houston Texans, threw for 527 yards in a 43-37 overtime victory over the Jacksonville Jaguars.

288. Jim Everett. Everett was selected with the 3rd overall pick in the 1986 draft by the Houston Oilers. The Oilers failed to sign him (Marvin Demoff was his agent) and ended up trading him to the Los Angeles Rams.

289. The Cleveland Browns selected Mike Phipps with the 3rd overall pick in the 1970 draft. The number one overall pick that year was Terry Bradshaw who was selected by the Pittsburgh Steelers. There were two other noteworthy selections in that first round. Al Cowlings, driver of O.J. Simpson's white Bronco, was selected with the 5th pick and Mike Reid, a two-time Pro Bowler, who would go on to write the song "Stranger in My House" popularized by Ronnie Milsap, was the 7th pick.

290. Drew Brees. Brees threw a touchdown in 54 consecutive regular season games setting the record during the 2012 season. Johnny Unitas was the previous record holder. Brees' streak ended against the Atlanta Falcons late that season. Tom Brady has a 52-game streak (ending in 2013) and Peyton Manning has a 51-game streak (ending in 2014). Of note, Brees also has a 45-game streak that began the week after his 54-game streak ended.

291. A.J. McCarron. McCarron threw for 9,017 yards for the Tide from 2010 to 2013. He was drafted in the 5th round by the Cincinnati Bengals and played 7 years as a backup.

292. Jack Kemp and Heath Shuler. Kemp, who quarterbacked several teams retired in 1969 after his last season with the Buffalo Bills. He had a very distinguished political career in Congress as well as serving as George H. W. Bush's Secretary of Housing and Urban Development. He also was the Vice-Presidential running

mate of Bob Dole in the 1996 election. Shuler was selected with the 3rd overall pick of the Washington Redskins in the 1994 draft. He retired in 1999. He served in Congress from 2007 to 2013.

293. Steve Sarkisian. Sarkisian won the Sammy Baugh Trophy in 1996 as the nation's top passer. He passed for 4,207 yards his senior year and was a second-team All American. He played 3 seasons for the Saskatchewan Roughriders in the CFL before turning to coaching. He now coaches the Texas Longhorns. John Beck played for the Miami Dolphins in 2007 and the Washington Redskins in 2011. Max Hall played for the Arizona Cardinals in 2010 and Steve Walsh played for the Cowboys, Saints, Bears, Rams, Buccaneers, and Colts from 1989 to 1999.

294. Vince Young. Young is 7th on that list. In order they are Warren Moon, Steve McNair, George Blanda, Dan Pastorini and Ryan Tannehill.

295. Aaron Rodgers. Rodgers' record for the Packers was 147-75-1 for a 65.9% win percentage. Favre, playing in 30 more games than Rodgers, had a win percentage of 63.2%. Bart Starr's win percentage was 59.9%. Each of the three had winning playoff records. Starr was 9-1, Favre was 13-11, and Rodgers was 11-10.

296. Ty Detmer. On September 23, 2001, Detmer, while playing for the Detroit Lions, threw 7 picks against the Cleveland Browns. The Browns won the game 24-14. Detmer was 22 of 42 for 212 yards, 1 touchdown and 7 interceptions. His counterpart, Tim Couch of the Browns, was 12 of 20 for 138 yards 3 touchdowns and 2 interceptions. Of Detmers 7 interceptions, 3 were to Browns rookie defensive back Anthony Henry who would end up with 10 picks for the year.

297. Joe Namath. Namath, while playing for the New York Jets, threw 6 interceptions against the Houston Oilers on October 15, 1967 (the game ended in a 28-28 tie), 6 interceptions against the Baltimore Colts on October 18, 1970 (Colts won 29-22), and 6 interceptions against the Miami Dolphins on October 19, 1975 (Miami won 43-0). There's something strange about the fact that all 3 games were played in mid-October.

298. Tom Tupa. Tupa, of Ohio State University, was selected in the 3$^{rd}$ round of the 1988 NFL draft by the Phoenix Cardinals. In his second season with the Cardinals, he started 2 games at quarterback. One of those games was against the Philadelphia Eagles on October 15, 1989. In that game Tupa was 16 of 41 for 266 yards, no touchdowns and 6 interceptions. The Eagles went on to defeat the Cardinals by a score of 17-5. The Eagles' Randall Cunningham would throw 3 interceptions of his own in that game. A couple other items of note: Tupa's 6 interceptions were to 6 different Eagle defenders while Cunningham's 3 were to 3 different Cardinal defenders. In all, 9 players got interceptions that day. And oh yeah, there were 4 fumbles that day, two for each team. And yes, all 4 were recovered by 4 different players. Tom Tupa would go on to become a Pro Bowl (1999) punter playing for several teams. He retired after the 2004 season.

299. Brady went undefeated in his career against the Minnesota Vikings (6-0), Tampa Bay Buccaneers (4-0), and New England Patriots (1-0).

300. The Denver Broncos were 9-9 in the regular season against Tom Brady but were 3-1 against him in the playoffs. In total, the Broncos' record against Brady was 12-10.

# Your kind words make a big difference!

If you found this book entertaining, educational, and fun to have around, will you please leave a review? Just scan the QR code below or, visit your Amazon orders page, find this book, and click "write a customer review".

Taking the couple extra minutes to leave a review is greatly appreciated.

## Thank you!

# *Acknowledgements*

Thank you to the love of my life Rachel, and my children Teale, Bridger, Lauryn and Henry. You are my constant source of joy and strength.

Special thanks to the Old Man's Club and its members, Brent Allen, Jeff Hayman, Scott Worthington, Tim McConnell, Tim McClintock, Erik Van Gaalen, Patrick Sai, and Brian Tavernas. You all inspired me to be creative in my thinking, focus on what's fun, and to dive ever deeper down the rabbit hole. Cheers to each one of you.

Thanks also to:
My fellow pig bandits and our memorable times together. We'll always have Chicago.

Jerry Kramer. I've been hooked on football since reading your book *Instant Replay* as a 9-year-old. It was the first book I ever read and is still my favorite.

Jack Thompson. You unknowingly inspired me to believe in me and to this day you are still my role model. GO COUGS!

## *About the Author*

TJ Johnson is a retired business executive living with his wife Rachel in central California. A Washington State University and University of Pennsylvania graduate, TJ loves his Seahawks, drinks Old Fashioneds and thinks of new trivia questions to share with anyone who will listen. His all-time favorite quarterback is Dan Marino.

www.ingramcontent.com/pod-product-compliance
Lightning Source LLC
Chambersburg PA
CBHW050910160426
43194CB00011B/2348